WHY DANTE MATTERS

WHY DANTE MATTERS

AN INTELLIGENT PERSON'S GUIDE

JOHN TOOK

BLOOMSBURY CONTINUUM
LONDON · OXFORD · NEW YORK · NEW DELHI · SYDNEY

BLOOMSBURY CONTINUUM
Bloomsbury Publishing Plc
50 Bedford Square, London, WC1B 3DP, UK

BLOOMSBURY, BLOOMSBURY CONTINUUM and the Diana logo are trademarks
of Bloomsbury Publishing Plc

First published in Great Britain 2020

A catalogue record for this book is available from the British Library

Library of Congress Cataloguing-in-Publication data has been applied for

ISBN: HB: 978-1-4729-5103-8; eBook: 978-1-4729-5104-5;
ePDF: 978-1-4729-5105-2

2 4 6 8 10 9 7 5 3 1

Typeset by Deanta Global Publishing Services, Chennai, India
Printed and bound in Great Britain by CPI Group (UK) Ltd, Croydon CR0 4YY

To find out more about our authors and books visit www.bloomsbury.com
and sign up for our newsletters

In memory of Kenelm Foster, OP (1910–86)

Spe sociae exultationis

It is indeed a question of whether the peculiar contemporaneousness of the work of art does not consist precisely in its being open in a limitless way to ever new integrations. The creator of a work of art may intend the public of his own time, but the real being of his work is what it is able to say, and this being reaches fundamentally beyond any historical confinement. In this sense, the work of art occupies a timeless present.

Hans-Georg Gadamer

The greatest poetic expression of the Existentialist point of view in the Middle Ages is Dante's *Divina Commedia*. It remains, like the religious depth psychology of the monastics, within the framework of the scholastic ontology. But within these limits it enters the deepest places of human self-destruction and despair as well as the highest places of courage and salvation, and gives in poetic symbols an all-embracing existential doctrine of man.

Paul Tillich

In fondo, una serietà terribile ...

Gianfranco Contini

CONTENTS

ACKNOWLEDGEMENTS

In addition to the many students both at University College London and latterly at the Warburg Institute who, having listened attentively, have by way of their generous response encouraged me to look ever more deeply into the matter, I have to thank Robin Baird-Smith of Bloomsbury Publishing for his kindness and courtesy in encouraging this project, and, as always, my wife Patricia for her companionship and forbearance.

Forse ancora per più sottile persona si vederebbe in ciò
più sottile ragione; ma questa è quella ch'io ne veggio, e
che più mi piace.

(*Vita nova* xxix.4)

Provided only that it deliver the goods, the Introduction following
hard upon the heels of this preface will, I hope, make it clear what
this fresh meditation on Dante sets out to do – namely to confirm
how it is that, over and beyond his status as a cultural asset and indeed
as a cultural icon, he still matters to us. The undertaking, I know, is
problematic, not least in that like all the great representatives of our
tradition – be it Shakespeare in the sphere of letters, Rembrandt
in the sphere of portraiture or Beethoven in the sphere of music –
Dante matters in as many different ways as those entering into his
presence. What follows, then, far from being yet another account
of his life and work, is simply my own sense of how it is that, every
more specifically historical consideration apart, he enters still into
communion with all those busy at the point of ultimate concern,
of what in truth it means to be under way on the plane of properly
human being. While, then, others of greater discerning may see
here matters of still greater moment, that is what I myself see and
that is what pleases me most.

John Took
University College London

INTRODUCTION:
DANTE AND THE EXISTENTIAL POINT OF VIEW

D ANTE AT THE POINT of ultimate concern – Dante: who, what, where and when? – course of the argument.

DANTE AT THE POINT OF ULTIMATE CONCERN

Why, then, does Dante matter?

In truth, for any number of reasons: for the theologian by way of his proceeding in terms not of the proposition pure and simple but of the agony and ecstasy of spiritual journeying, of the I-self anxious in respect of his or her coming home as a creature of ultimate accountability; for the philosopher by way of his particular brand of Christian Aristotelianism and of the possibility this holds out of a unique form of properly human happiness here and now; and for the rhetorician by way of his sense of the word as but the intelligible form of this or that instance of specifically human being in act and of the image not now as a matter of elaboration or adornment in respect of the plain sense of the text, but as a first port of call when it comes to laying open the *how it stands and how it fares* with the individual (Martin Heidegger's 'wie einem ist und wird') at the point of self-losing and self-finding.

But to speak in this way of what amounts to the high-level concerns of the text – to a setting up of the theological issue, that is to say, in terms of the more or less anxious I-self, of the philosophical preferences of the day, and of the word and of the image as that whereby the individual knows self and is in turn known in the truth of his or her presence in the world as a creature of moral and intellectual determination – is already to point on to what actually and ultimately matters about the Dantean utterance, namely its taking up of every specifically cultural inflexion of the spirit in a meditation upon the positive *being there* of the individual in the fullness of his or her proper humanity. Short of this – of this commitment to the *being there* of self in the fullness of its proper humanity and to this as but the first and final cause of every spiritual striving – the text lives on as a matter merely of historical interest, as but the more or less predictable product of its immediate circumstances. Sensitive, by contrast, to – as Dante himself puts it at one point – the "butterfly-emergence" of the one who says 'I', it straightaway transcends those circumstances in favour of something still more resplendent, of a nothing if not lively encounter with all those – past, present and as yet unborn – engaged at the point of ultimate concern.

DANTE: WHO, WHAT, WHERE AND WHEN?

But with this we are getting ahead of ourselves, for if only by way of honouring the kind of otherness always and everywhere entering into sameness as the condition of good conversation we need to pause for a moment over Dante himself, over the *who, what, where* and *when* of his own presence in the world.

Dante was born in Florence in 1265 under the sign of Gemini to a White Guelph family of erstwhile comfortable though in recent times of more modest means. Of his childhood and early education we have little to go on other than by way of inference and probability: of inference in the sense of a child doubtless more than ordinarily responsive to the sights and sounds both of the city and of the Florentine countryside and of this as making in turn for a lively imagination and love of myth and of mythmaking, and of probability in the sense of a preliminary initiation in the area of reading, writing and arithmetic with access further down the line to texts such as the *Disticha Catonis* or the *Liber Esopi* or the *Elegia* of Arrigo Settimello as likewise part of an elementary curriculum. But more decisive still, certainly as time went on, was the personal encounter, the presence to him of the poet, encyclopaedist and civic dignitary Brunetto Latini and of the poet and philosopher Guido Cavalcanti, the former in respect of a certain kind of pre-humanism or preliminary encounter with the poets, philosophers and rhetoricians of old, and the latter in respect both of the style and of the substance of versifying in the vernacular, both of the accountability of form to content within the economy of the whole and of the precise nature of love in its twofold substance and psychology. But neither, as far as his formation as a philosophical spirit was concerned, was that all, for in the wake of Beatrice's death in June 1290 (a matter to which we shall come in due course) he sought consolation in the theological schools of Santa Maria Novella, of Santa Croce and, on the other side of the river, of Santo Spirito, the sermons, lectures and disputations thereof – respectively Dominican, Franciscan and Augustinian in complexion – serving further to shape and substantiate his ever more complex spirituality.

Meanwhile events moved on apace on the domestic, the military and the civic fronts. On the domestic front there was the death of his mother Bella somewhere between 1270 and 1275 and of his father Alighiero in either 1280 or 1281, at which point responsibility for the estate, such as it was, fell principally on Dante himself, though on a Dante generously assisted in this respect by his brother Francesco, a friend in need at every stage along the way. And then too there was his betrothal in January 1277 to Gemma Donati of the powerful Black Guelph family in Florence, to whom he was married possibly in 1285 and by whom he had three or maybe four children – Pietro, Jacopo, Antonia and, again maybe, a Giovanni as his first-born son. On the military front, by contrast, there were the twin actions of Caprona and of Campaldino towards the end of that same decade, the former furnishing some of the martial imagery of the *Inferno* and the latter, according to a letter no longer extant but seen by Leonardo Bruni, marking the beginning, Dante says, of his every misfortune on the political stage of Florence. More obviously decisive, however, as the beginning of that misfortune was his enrolment, probably in 1295, in the Guild of Apothecaries and Physicians as a first step towards serving on the governing councils of the city and, by 1300, on the priorate itself as its supreme legislative organ, by which time, however, the prospect of a Black Guelph *coup d'état* aided and abetted by both the papacy and the House of Anjou loomed more than ever large. Versions of Dante's precise whereabouts during the unspeakable violence of November 1301 vary, but however that may be he must have fled the city by the end of January 1302, for by then he had been condemned *in absentia* for, among other things, fraudulence in public office, and, by March of the same year, to be burnt alive should he be taken upon Florentine soil.

Exile for Dante, as perhaps exile always is, was a scarcely less than agonizing experience, each successive inflexion of the spirit being qualified in the self-same moment by its polar counterpart: heroism by a sense of humiliation and of the hopelessness of it all, resolve by resignation, and resilience by an inkling of repentance, all this making at another level of consciousness for a resurgence of courage and for a need to define afresh the reasons of his existence. Sustained even so, for the moment at any rate, by hopes for a speedy return thanks to the good offices of Cardinal Nicolò da Prato as peacemaker he withdrew to Verona where he was hosted by Bartolomeo della Scala as prominent among his patrons in exile. But the Black Guelph administration in Florence was more than equal to the cardinal's plan for a more inclusive administration, Dante for his part, having conferred in vain with his colleagues in Arezzo relative to a speedy resolution of it all, making his lonely way back to the Scaligeri in Verona. True, the imperial adventuring of Henry VII of Luxembourg held out fresh possibility for a return, but what with his naïveté relative to Italian and especially Florentine civic scheming, his near-astonishing lack of proper preparation and his death in August 1313 it all came to nothing, Dante thereafter repairing afresh to Verona as the guest this time of the Cangrande della Scala nobly lauded in the *Paradiso*. True too that something approaching an amnesty was offered by the Florentines in the course of 1315 ("something approaching" in that there was here no mention of Dante by name), an offer which, having by this stage redefined the parameters of his existence (the "may I not anywhere gaze upon the face of the sun and of the stars" of his response to the offer), he dismissed as unworthy both of his name and of his suffering. Before long, therefore, and at the invitation of the kindly Guido Novello, he found a fresh home in Ravenna, where until the hour of his death in 1321 he was both honoured as a poet, scholar and diplomat and comforted by the presence to him of some at least of his family.

Coming, then – but for the moment with comparable brevity – to his accomplishment as by turns, and indeed latterly in one and the same moment, poet, philosopher, pedagogue and prophet, we may begin by saying that, having experimented in the tradition of Siculo-Tuscan versemaking going back to the court of Frederick II of Hohenstaufen in Palermo, Dante, in the first of his major works – the *Vita nova* dating in an ideal chronology from somewhere between 1293 and 1295 – settled on a *prosimetrum* designed by way of its prose component to clarify the circumstances and significance of certain at least of his lyric poems. Ostensibly – and to the deep reasons of the *Vita nova* as a meditation upon the nature and finality of love as but a principle of radical self-transcendence on the part of the conscientious lover we shall in a moment return – the text offers an account of Dante's experience of Beatrice as, precisely, a bringer of blessing, and this from his first encounter with her as a child all the way through to, and beyond, her premature death in 1290. First, then, comes the childhood and youthful encounter and Beatrice's first greeting of the poet, an encounter marked from the outset by the tremulousness and indeed by the trauma of it all and yet at the same time by the ecstasy and transformative power of the epiphanous presence. In consequence, however, of a moment of misunderstanding (Dante had resorted to the strategy of 'screen ladies' or intermediary figures for the purposes of maintaining a proper decorum), Beatrice saw fit to deny her greeting, at which point Dante, confused by the power of love both to delight and to distress, set about rethinking the whole thing, about redefining love as a matter not so much of *acquisition* as of *disposition*, of – by way precisely of praise as a matter of standing in the presence of the other and of the greater than self – knowing self in the ever more ample substance of self. The idea, however, was easier to contemplate than to live out, for no sooner had Beatrice died than the seeds of temptation were sown by the sight of one looking kindly upon him, by a 'donna gentile' or 'gracious lady of the casement' appearing in her compassion to hold out the possibility of a surrogate happiness, of, more exactly (for the psychology of it all is nicely complex), a way back to Beatrice in the flesh. Once more, then, Dante's was a state of spiritual turmoil, a crisis of conscience admitting of resolution by way only of a fresh vision of Beatrice in glory and of a steady commitment to speak no more of her until such time as learning, wisdom and a more complete insight into the meaning of it all was properly his.

Dante's, then, was from the beginning an exploration both of the dialectics and of the deepening substance of his experience as a poet and philosopher, the first of these things, the dialectical component of his spirituality, enjoying vigorous expression in the so-called *rime petrose* or 'stony rhymes' of the middle part or thereabouts of the 1290s. Here, certainly, it is a question of the triumph of possession over disposition, the now impossible difficulty and intractability of his love making only for its violent to the point of orgiastic resolution, for a more or less violent imposition of self upon madonna as but the cause of his frustration and despair. No less committed, however, and, with it, no less eloquent are those now specifically moral *rime* dating from much the same time and looking somewhat after the manner of Brunetto Latini to educate Dante's chosen readership in the ways and means of true nobility and social elegance, essays, these, in the civilizing substance of the poetic line and destined eventually to find their way into the alas incomplete *Convivio* or *Banquet* of his early years in exile.

The incompletion of the *Convivio*, a work dating in an again ideal chronology from about 1304 to 1307 and by its own account a response to the catastrophe of that exile, is in fact of the essence, for here especially the tension generated by Dante's successive and indeed simultaneous spiritual allegiances – by, in short, his commitment both to a species of philosophical idealism making for an ecstatic resolution of self on the plane of seeing, understanding and desiring and, in the very same moment, to a species of Peripateticism making for an abrupt shortening of the spiritual perspective – moves centre-stage, its magnanimity thus surrendering at last to the fragility of the project, to a foundering of the text upon its own leading emphases. Ostensibly, then, what we have here is but a partial implementation of the original idea, just four books of the fifteen originally envisaged, but four books pulsating all the same with an unmistakable Dantean energy, with an unwavering commitment to the urgency of the matter to hand. Perfectly exquisite, therefore, is the first book with its sturdy commitment to – as Dante himself suggests in its twilight moments – a fresh feeding of the five thousand, of those "many men and women in this language of ours burdened by domestic and civic care" and to that extent living on at a remove from their proper humanity. No less urgent, however, when it comes to the aforesaid philosophical idealism are Books II and III, where it is a question now of philosophy understood as but the love of wisdom coeval and consubstantial with the Godhead and as making in man for a radical assimilation of the creature to the creator, for a fresh making over of the former in the likeness and image of the latter. And then finally, as the first course proper of Dante's banquet (everything so far being but an hors d'oeuvre) comes an account in Book IV of the true nature of nobility, of *gentilezza* as a matter less of wealth, manners and social lineage than – much after the manner of the night sky as host to its many bright stars – of the encompassing of every moral and intellectual virtue in man, of his every discrete striving of the spirit. Again, however, it is with the ascendancy especially of Aristotle as if not the founder then the finisher of the entire art and science of moral philosophy that the difficulty and, with it, the ultimate impossibility of the *Convivio* as a stable expression of Dante's complex spirituality commends itself as an object of contemplation, the *Convivio* – the nothing if not large-souled *Convivio* – thus living on in anticipation of something still greater to come.

If, however, by the magnanimity or 'large-souledness' of the text we mean its preoccupation less with the idea pure and simple than with those to whom that same idea is present as a principle of properly human well-being and thus of properly human happiness, then what applies to the *Convivio* applies also to the ideally contemporary *De vulgari eloquentia* and to the *Monarchia* as dating probably from the middle of the second decade of the fourteenth century, from – probably – 1314 or 1315.

Taking to begin with, then, the *De vulgari eloquentia*, here again we have yet another text incomplete by virtue of its incompletability, of its gradually being overtaken by the more ample and inclusive linguistic and literary sensibility of the *Commedia* as now shaping up in Dante's mind. First, in Book I, comes the linguistic aspect of his meditation, his reaching out by way (*a*) of a now secure sense of the unique nobility of – *vis-à-vis* Latin – the vernacular as the primary and connatural means in man of spiritual intelligence, (*b*) of a nicely detailed account of the linguistic diaspora contingent upon Babel and of the linguistic geography of Europe as a whole, and (*c*) of a nothing if not spirited review of the currently spoken forms of Italian up and down the peninsula for a *vulgare illustre* or illustrious vernacular whereby a certain set of people at a certain stage of their socio-political and economic development might know themselves in the distinctiveness of their proper humanity, in the unique *italianitas* of their proper presence in the world. Next, in Book II, comes an account of specifically poetic form as a matter not now of addition or of decoration where the plain sense of the text is concerned but rather as that whereby the would-be poet in the high style knows himself in the twofold truth and soaring substance of his proper humanity. Now to speak in this way of an 'illustrious vernacular' and of the 'would-be poet in the high style' is at once to underline the exclusivity of it all, of its straightaway ruling out the linguistic legitimacy of anything approaching the merely local or (as Dante himself puts it) the 'municipal' and the poetic legitimacy of anything approaching the merely meretricious or stylistically untoward, and it is precisely this exclusivity that accounts for and confirms the eclipse of the *De vulgari eloquentia* as Dante's last word in the area of language and of literary aesthetics. But for all that, its generosity and indeed its greatness of spirit live on intact, for this, no less than the *Vita nova* and the *Convivio* before it and the

Commedia after it, is an essay in the ontologization of the matter to hand, in the bringing home of form – be it linguistic or literary – to the individual or the group of individuals as that whereby he, she or they might stand securely in their own presence as creatures of orderly being and becoming.

More readily open to interpretation in terms of the tradition in which it stands – in terms, that is to say, of the tradition of publicistic literature reaching back to and indeed beyond the Investiture Contest of the eleventh century and turning upon the relationship between the prince and the pope within the economy of the whole – is the *Monarchia*, conceived probably in the wake of Henry VII's demise in August 1313 and belonging therefore to the middle years of that decade. Taken in the round the work constitutes a nothing if not sustained account of the Roman idea pure and simple, of, more exactly, the prior and subsistent necessity of the Roman imperial project as the ground and guarantee of peace, piety and prosperity in Christendom as a whole. Straightaway, therefore, it is a question of the indispensability of monarchy or of government by one to man's proper perfection as man, to (as far as society as a whole is concerned) the total actualization of the possible intellect or of his collective power to orderly understanding and (as far as the individual is concerned) the free passage from seeing and understanding to being and doing, to knowing self, that is to say, in the freedom of self. Then, in Book II, comes a no less systematic statement of that same indispensability under its Roman aspect, Rome no less than Jerusalem figuring from beforehand as the instrument of divine willing, of God's plan for man as a creature of moral, intellectual and ultimately eschatological accountability. And finally, in Book III, comes the properly polemical moment of the *Monarchia*, polemical to the point of gladiatorial (Dante's own expression on the threshold of the book) in its commitment (*a*) to a step-by-step dismantling of the long since hallowed forms and formularies of papal hierocratic consciousness (few of them, he thinks, standing up to scrutiny), and (*b*) to a programme of political dualism, to the notion of man as having by nature two ultimate ends (the temporal and the eternal), two means to those ends (the moral and the theological virtues respectively), and thus two authorities – the prince and the pope – to confirm him in his proper well-being here and hereafter. And it is at this point that the existential intensity of the text yet again shines through as its innermost and abiding substance, for what matters ultimately about the precise configuration of princely and papal power in Europe is its function as the in-and-through-which of man's proper well-being as man, as that whereby both the individual and the group to which he or she belongs, and indeed mankind in the totality thereof, might rejoice at last in the twofold fullness and freedom of their proper humanity.

With this, then, we come to the miracle that is the *Commedia*, to a miracle in the sense that what we have here, in a single pass of the mind and imagination, is (*a*) a confessional statement at once opening out onto the fully and unequivocally prophetic, (*b*) an account of the substance and psychology of human being under the conditions of time and eternity second to none in point of power and precision, (*c*) a now fully immanent eschatology such that what a man *will be* under the aspect of eternity he already *is* under the aspect of time, and (*d*) a final and indeed triumphant vindication of the image as the in-and-through-which of spiritual intelligence, as uniquely adequate to the matter in hand. Dante, then, as protagonist in his own poem and thus speaking in the first person, finds himself, in the midst of his days, astray in a dark wood, the straight way being lost. Anxious, therefore, to make his escape to the sunlit uplands beyond but prey to the inexplicability and fearfulness of it all, he discerns a shadowy figure turning out to be the great Roman poet Virgil who, as himself a singer of exile and homecoming, summons him to an alternative journey: to a descent into the pit there to behold the endless forms of self-betrayal and thus of spiritual disfiguration as but the downside of man's proper power to moral self-determination; to an ascent of Mount Purgatory there to witness the struggle of the penitent spirit to affirm self over self on the plane of properly human loving; and finally to a crossing of the circling spheres of Dante's geocentric universe there to encounter as but the ground and guarantee of his own being and becoming the One who *is* as of the essence. While, then, at every stage of the journey Dante the protagonist in his own poem looks on and learns, Dante the author and architect of the poem reconstructs with again perfect power and precision an entire trajectory of human experience, foregrounding as he does so the agony and ecstasy of it all: the despair of those intent upon delivering themselves to the self-consciously inauthentic project (the infernal phase of the journey); the travail of those busy at the point of love-harvesting, of bringing home every occasional instance of human loving to the love given with the act itself of existence (the purgatorial phase of the journey); and the perfect peace, not to mention the perfect joy, of those now standing securely in their own company as 'creatures capable of the creator' (the paradisal phase of the journey).

And then finally, as testifying no less fervently to the vernacularity both of his own being and by extension – albeit implicitly – to the vernacularity of human being in general, to the role of one's native tongue as a principle not merely of intelligibility but of self-intelligibility, we have the eclogues forming part of a correspondence inaugurated by the scholar and proto-humanist Giovanni del Virgilio and belonging now to the twilight years of Dante's life. But for all the still terrifying seriousness of the text, this is terrifying seriousness worn lightly, seriousness testifying now to a state of superlative self-possession. Has not the time come, says his illustrious correspondent, to set aside the albeit egregious substance of his versemaking to date in favour of something good and literary in Latin, of an epic account of the deeds and accomplishments of, say, a Henry VII of Luxembourg or a Cangrande della Scala, a certainty, this, for the laurel crown. Dante, doubtless, was impressed, but entering more than ever graciously into the spirit of the thing he will, he says (by the bye in nicely Latin bucolics), send on instead ten measures of milk from the choicest of his herd – ten cantos, doubtless, of the sublime *Paradiso* – content meanwhile to sup upon the oaten fare simmering gently in their rustic tabernacle:

> Tunc ego: "Cum mundi circumflua corpora cantu
> astricoleque meo, velut infera regna, patebunt,
> devincire caput hedera lauroque iuvabit:

concedat Mopsus". "Mopsus" tunc ille "quid?" inquit.
"Comica nonne vides ipsum reprehendere verba,
tum quia femineo resonant ut trita labello,
tum quia Castalias pudet acceptare sorores?"
ipse ego respondi, versus iterumque relegi,
Mopse, tuos. Tunc ille humeros contraxit et "Ergo
quid faciemus" ait "Mopsum revocare volentes?".
"Est mecum quam noscis ovis gratissima," dixi
"ubera vix que ferre potest, tam lactis abundans;
rupe sub ingenti carptas modo ruminat herbas.
Nulli iuncta gregi nullis assuetaque caulis,
sponte venire solet, nunquam vi, poscere mulctram.
Hanc ego prestolor manibus mulgere paratis,
hac implebo decem missurus vascula Mopso.
Tu tamen interdum capros meditere petulcos
et duris crustis discas infigere dentes".
Talia sub quercu Melibeus et ipse canebam,
parva tabernacla nobis dum farra coquebant.

Then I: "When the bodies that flow round the world, and
they that dwell among the stars, shall be shown forth in my
song, even as the lower realms, then shall I joy to bind my
brow with ivy and with laurel, if Mopsus will but allow."
"What then of Mopsus?" he replied. "Seest thou not how he
blames the words of the Comedy in that they all sound trite
on women's lips, and that the Castalian sisters think scorn
to accept them?" So did I answer him; and once again I read
thy verses, Mopsus. Whereon he shrugged his shoulders and
replied: "What then to do would we win Mopsus to our side?"
"I have," said I, "one sheep, thou knowest, most loved; so full
of milk she may scarce bear her udders; even now under a
mighty rock she chews the late-cropped grass. Associate with
no flock, familiar to no pen, of her own will she forever comes,
ne'er must be driven to the milking-pail. Her do I think to
milk with ready hands; from her ten measures I will fill and
send to Mopsus. Do thou meanwhile think on thy wanton

goats and learn to ply thy teeth on stubborn crusts." Such strains under an oak did I and Meliboeus sing, the whilst our little hut was cooking our barley.

(*Eclogue* II.48–68)

COURSE OF THE ARGUMENT

Dante's, whatever else it is, is a steady engagement at the level of specifically cultural concern, a steady preoccupation, that is to say, with the leading issues – be they theological, philosophical, linguistic or literary-aesthetic in kind – of the day, and a steady negotiation with the leading lights of the traditions in which he stands. Theologically, then, it is a question of his rejoicing in the at once Augustinian, Dominican and Franciscan components of his spirituality, in the psychology and phenomenology of far-wandering traceable to the Bishop of Hippo, in the genius for orderly exposition proper to Thomas, and in the by turns, and indeed often enough simultaneously, renunciatory and reformist spirit of those who, like Francis, saw themselves as but the latter-day representatives of Christ's poor. Philosophically, by contrast, it is a question of his rejoicing in the kind of Peripateticism or neo-Aristotelianism progressively decisive for the substance and structure of human experience in its moment-by-moment unfolding, while linguistically and rhetorically it is a question of his pondering the power and persuasiveness of the classical utterance for everything coming next by way of the vernacular initiative, the latter, he thought, wanting for nothing in point of sweet *concinnitas*.

But this steady engagement at the level of specifically cultural concern notwithstanding, what we have in Dante – and this now is what matters – is a bringing home of each of these things, of each successive emphasis in the area of theology, philosophy, language and literature, to the existential issue as the encompassing, as the whereabouts of its proper functionality. This situation is everywhere discernible in the text and everywhere decisive for its interpretation. It is discernible in the *Vita nova* as the great work of Dante's early years where it is a question of love properly understood – of love, that is to say, as a matter less of possession than of praise – as that whereby the lover knows himself in the kind of 'transhumanity' (the 'trasumanar' of *Paradiso* I.70) as but humanity itself in its proper coming about. It is discernible in the *Convivio* in its preoccupation not merely nor even primarily with the routine emphases of classical and medieval philosophy precisely as such, but with a love of wisdom making in its espousal for a more ample and indeed for a more authentic species both of private and of collective self-affirmation. It is discernible in the first book of the ideally contemporary *De vulgari eloquentia* in its seeking out and settling upon an ideal form of the Italian vernacular as that whereby a new Latin race rejoices in its proper distinctiveness, and it is discernible in the second book of the *De vulgari eloquentia* in its preoccupation not now with the legerdemain of classical and late medieval rhetoricism but with the poetic utterance as the means of a now soaring spirit, as that whereby the would-be poet in the high style knows himself as beloved of the gods. It is discernible in the *Monarchia* where, for all its publicistic complexion, it is a question of Rome in all its latter-day resurrection as but the ground and guarantee of a full, free and flourishing humanity, and it is discernible in the *Commedia* where by way of a nothing if not arduous process of self-confrontation, of self-reconfiguration and of self-transcendence the soul knows itself at last in its properly ecstatic substance, its proper coming forth on the planes of knowing and loving.

It is this, therefore, this constant referral in Dante of the cultural to the existential as always and everywhere a matter of ultimate concern, that determines the shape and substance of what comes next in these pages. First, then, and by way of preparation for a close encounter with the text proper, comes an account of – as Dante himself understands it – self and selfhood in respect (*a*) of its theological and ethical profile, (*b*) of the structures of consciousness proper to man as he seeks to bring home the occasional to the ontological on the plane of seeing, understanding and desiring (being as *ahead* of itself, as *away* from itself, and, by way of conscience as but a matter of *with-knowing*, as *alongside* itself), and (*c*) of a phenomenology of being, of the *mood* of this or that instance of specifically human being as transparent to the *truth* of that being. Following on from this, and constituting the main business of the book, comes a meditation on the *Vita nova*, on the *Convivio* and on the *Commedia* as, each after its manner, an essay in ontic emancipation, of the freeing of self for the proper fullness of self. And finally, as on the face of it a corollary but in truth as entering into the mainstream of the argument, comes a review of the specifically linguistic dimension of the matter, language, both in its unadorned and in its musical and rhetorical elaboration, testifying in Dante's sense of it to the status of this or that individual man or woman as fully and unequivocally *there* in the world, as present to self in point both of actuality and of intelligibility. No language, no presence. Merely possibility.

Dante, Self and Selfhood

L OVE-PROCESSION AND THE LOVE-IMPERATIVE:
preliminary considerations in the areas of theology and
ethics – patterns of self-relatedness: being as *ahead* of self, as *away*
from self and *alongside* self – a phenomenology of being.

LOVE-PROCESSION AND THE LOVE-IMPERATIVE: PRELIMINARY CONSIDERATIONS IN THE AREAS OF THEOLOGY AND ETHICS

At the beginning of Dante's meditation as a poet – indeed as *the* poet
in European letters – of specifically human being and becoming
stands the One who *is* as of the essence, the God of the old and
new dispensation, the One who, suffering in his self-sufficiency
no addition, subsists beyond the structures of time and space as
the leading paradigms of human awareness. All circumscribing but
uncircumscribed and a stranger to every material co-ordinate, he
comprehends – in the sense of containing within himself – every
kind of substance and accident, every modality of being either as
possibility or actuality. Perfectly centred in respect of his own being,
he knows himself and is known by way of a continuous process
of love-overflowing, the stasis or stillness of the Godhead thus
coinciding with the most complete kind of *ec*stasis or coming forth;
so, for example, on the unity and undividedness of the Godhead,
these lines (142–45) from Canto XXIX of the *Paradiso*:

> Vedi l'eccelso omai e la larghezza
> de l'etterno valor, poscia che tanti

speculi fatti s'ha in che si spezza,
uno manendo in sé come davanti.

Behold the height and breadth of the eternal goodness in that, having made of itself so many mirrors wherein it is dispersed, it yet remains, in itself, one and undivided.

while on God as the encompassing, as the uncircumscribed but all-circumscribing principle of everything that *is* in the universe, these lines (1–6 and 28–30 respectively) from *Purgatorio* XI and *Paradiso* XIV:

> O Padre nostro, che ne' cieli stai,
> non circunscritto, ma per più amore
> ch'ai primi effetti di là sù tu hai,
> laudato sia 'l tuo nome e 'l tuo valore
> da ogne creatura, com' è degno
> di render grazie al tuo dolce vapore
> …
> Quell' uno e due e tre che sempre vive
> e regna sempre in tre e 'n due e 'n uno,
> non circunscritto, e tutto circunscrive …

Our Father, who art in heaven, not circumscribed, but by reason of the surpassing love you bear your first works on high, hallowed be your name and your great goodness by every creature, it being meet and right to give thanks for your sweet exhalation … that one, two and three which ever lives and ever reigns three, two and one, uncircumscribed and all-circumscribing …

and on the Godhead as containing without prejudice to its simplicity every kind of substantial and accidental form in the created order, these lines (85–90) from *Paradiso* XXXIII:

> Nel suo profondo vidi che s'interna,
> legato con amore in un volume,

> ciò che per l'universo si squaderna:
> sustanze e accidenti e lor costume
> quasi conflati insieme, per tal modo
> che ciò ch'i' dico è un semplice lume.

In its depth I saw ingathered, bound by love in a single volume, the universe unfolded, substances, accidents and their relations fused as it were one with another, yet in my telling of it but a simple light.

On the notion, by contrast, of God's forever opening out in fresh instances of creative and recreative concern – actuality thus being in him a matter of affectivity, of self as reaching out in love to inaugurate and sustain the other-than-self – these (lines 13–18) from *Paradiso* XXIX:

> Non per aver a sé di bene acquisto,
> ch'esser non può, ma perché suo splendore
> potesse, risplendendo, dir '*Subsisto*',
>   in sua etternità di tempo fore,
> fuor d'ogne altro comprender, come i piacque,
> s'aperse in nuovi amor l'etterno amore.

Not for gain of good unto itself, which cannot be, but that his splendour might, in its resplendence, say '*I AM*', the eternal love, knowing neither time nor any other context, at its pleasure opened out in yet new loves.

Throughout, then, the pattern is the same, for throughout it is a question of God's knowing himself not merely in the twofold simplicity and complexity of his being, of his comprehending without prejudice to the irreducibility of that being everything that ever was or ever will be by way of substance and of accident, but in the twofold self-possession and self-overflowing thereof as all of a piece within the sublime economy of the whole.

But with this we are as yet in the foothills, for the overflowing of the One in forever new orders of creative concern issues in the case of man, Dante thinks, in something as singular as it is stupendous, to wit, in each and every individual as a new creation and as empowered in respect both of its proximate and of its ultimate finalities. Taking the argument step by step, then, we may say this, that Dante's, when it comes to the theology of creation as a whole, is an amalgamation of primary and secondary causality, of God's enlisting the angels or Intelligences for the purpose of actualizing the idea pure and simple as present to the divine mind; so, for example, these lines from early on in the *Paradiso* with their nicely Platonizing – or, more exactly, Neoplatonizing – sense of the idea as received from on high and as modulated here below by those same Intelligences as responsible within the economy of the whole for its positive implementation:

> Dentro dal ciel de la divina pace
> si gira un corpo ne la cui virtute
> l'esser di tutto suo contento giace.
>   Lo ciel seguente, c'ha tante vedute,
> quell' esser parte per diverse essenze,
> da lui distratte e da lui contenute.
>   Li altri giron per varie differenze
> le distinzion che dentro da sé hanno
> dispongono a lor fini e lor semenze.
>   Questi organi del mondo così vanno,
> come tu vedi omai, di grado in grado,
> che di sù prendono e di sotto fanno.

Within the heaven of divine peace whirls a body in whose virtue lies the being of all it contains. The next heaven, with all its many lights, distributes this being essence by essence, each alike distinct from it and yet contained by it. The other circling heavens thus variously dispose the distinctions borne within them in respect of their proper fruit and finality, which organs of the universe, as now you see, proceed step by step, receiving from above and fashioning below.

(*Paradiso* II.112–23)

– lines to which, for the sake of confirming a now developed sense in Dante of the nature and extent of divine creativity precisely as such we ought for the record to add this now in part familiar passage from the other end of the *Paradiso* with its sense of that same creativity as extending in the first instance only to pure form, to pure matter and to the coalescence of these things in the circling spheres, everything else being in the way we have seen down to the angelic Intelligences as but the agents of God's prior purposes:

> Non per aver a sé di bene acquisto,
> ch'esser non può, ma perché suo splendore
> potesse, risplendendo, dir '*Subsisto*',
>   in sua etternità di tempo fore,
> fuor d'ogne altro comprender, come i piacque,
> s'aperse in nuovi amor l'etterno amore.
>   Né prima quasi torpente si giacque;
> ché né prima né poscia procedette
> lo discorrer di Dio sovra quest' acque.
>   Forma e materia, congiunte e purette,
> usciro ad esser che non avia fallo,
> come d'arco tricordo tre saette.
>   E come in vetro, in ambra o in cristallo
> raggio resplende sì, che dal venire
> a l'esser tutto non è intervallo,
>   così 'l triforme effetto del suo sire
> ne l'esser suo raggiò insieme tutto
> sanza distinzïone in essordire.
>   Concreato fu ordine e costrutto
> a le sustanze; e quelle furon cima
> nel mondo in che puro atto fu produtto;
>   pura potenza tenne la parte ima;
> nel mezzo strinse potenza con atto
> tal vime, che già mai non si divima.

Not for gain of good unto itself, which cannot be, but that his splendour might, in its resplendence, say '*I AM*', the eternal love, knowing neither time nor any other context, at its pleasure opened out in yet new loves. Nor before, as if inert, did he lie, for until his moving upon these waters there was no before or after. Like three arrows from a three-stringed bow, form and matter, simple and compound, came into being unblemished; and just as with glass, amber or crystal a ray passing through shines entire in the moment of its issuing, so did the threefold activity of their sovereign lord flash forth into being, the product of but a moment. Therewith came about the order and intelligibility of the separate substances, of those dwelling on high as but pure form. Down below was pure potentiality, with, between them, act and potentiality bound up one with the other indissociably.

(Paradiso XXIX.13–36)

This, then, is what it means to speak of Dante's combining in a single breath patterns of primary and secondary causality as the means of divine purposefulness in the world; for if on the one hand he is committed to the notion of God's bringing forth something from nothing as a matter of the affectivity all of a piece with his very being, he is on the other sufficiently enamoured of the Neoplatonic idea to admit it as a matter not simply of aesthetic but of cosmological interest, as a way of accommodating and accounting for the co-subsistence within the economy of being as a whole both of the one and of the many, both of sameness and of difference as ways of seeing and understanding the world.

But – and this now is what matters – when it comes to man it is quite different, for when it comes to man it is a question of God's direct intervention with a view to fashioning a creature after his own image, a creature, that is to say, fully present to self as a matter of concern and thus circling steadily about the still centre of its being. Again the key passages are worth reading over in full. First, then, and rejoicing not only in the notion of the Godhead as but a matter of self-overflowing in point of affective energy but in the likeness of the creature to the creator in point of proper freedom, of its accountability to none but the One from whom all being proceeds, we have these lines from *Paradiso* VII, the – as it happens – soteriological canto *par excellence* of the *Commedia*:

> La divina bontà, che da sé sperne
> ogne livore, ardendo in sé, sfavilla
> sì che dispiega le bellezze etterne.
> Ciò che da lei sanza mezzo distilla
> non ha poi fine, perché non si move
> la sua imprenta quand' ella sigilla.
> Ciò che da essa sanza mezzo piove
> libero è tutto, perché non soggiace
> a la virtute de le cose nove.
> Più l'è conforme, e però più le piace;
> ché l'ardor santo ch'ogne cosa raggia,
> ne la più somigliante è più vivace.

The divine goodness, which eschews all meanness, burns within itself such that in its sparkling it shows forth its eternal beauty. Whatever comes forth immediately from it has thenceforth no end, since its impress, once imposed, fades not. Those things raining down from it without intermediary, knowing no subjection to the merely made, are wholly free. Like as they are all the more to that goodness, so also are they the more pleasing to it; for the holy ardour that irradiates all things is all the livelier in whatever most resembles it.

(*Paradiso* VII.64–75)

This, then – this sense of God's rejoicing in the likeness of the creature to the creator and, with it, in something approaching their proper companionship – is Dante's point of departure when it comes to the status of man in particular as, with each individual, a new creation, a fresh product of divine purposefulness. Preliminary, therefore, in respect of a still more radiant expression of the idea in the *Purgatorio*, are these lines from the fourth book of the *Convivio*, preliminary indeed, but settled even so in their sense of God's turning back upon the handiwork of nature – upon the generation of the sensitive soul *ex materia* or by way of the normal process of procreation – with a view to *inspiring* or breathing into it the rational soul proper:

> E però dico che quando l'umano seme cade nel suo recettaculo, cioè ne la matrice, esso porta seco la vertù de l'anima generativa e la vertù del cielo e la vertù de li elementi legati, cioè la complessione; e matura e dispone la materia a la vertù formativa, la quale diede l'anima del generante; e la vertù formativa prepara li organi a la vertù celestiale, che produce de la potenza del seme l'anima in vita. La quale, incontanente produtta, riceve da la vertù del motore del cielo lo intelletto possibile; lo quale potenzialmente in sé adduce tutte le forme universali, secondo che sono nel suo produttore, e tanto meno quanto più dilungato da la prima Intelligenza è.

> It is my contention, then, that when the human seed enters the womb, it bears with it a threefold power: the power of the soul generating it, that of the heavens, and that of its elements as bound up one with another within the economy of the whole. It ripens and readies matter to receive the formative power deriving from the male parent, and this same formative power in turn prepares the organs to receive that of the heavens which from the potentiality of the seed produces the living soul. As soon as that soul is created, it receives from the mover of the heavens and the power thereof the possible intellect, this in turn having the capacity to receive into itself (though in a manner proportionate to its distance from the first mind) every kind of universal form as present to its maker.

> (*Convivio* IV.xxi.4–5)

while as more properly hymnic in their celebration of the divine initiative in respect of the rational soul we have these lines from the *Purgatorio*, lines more than ordinarily exquisite in their sense of an order of being – that of man himself as an immediate product of divine intentionality – turning gently about the still centre of its at once unique and uniquely precious presence in the world:

> Apri a la verità che viene il petto;
> e sappi che, sì tosto come al feto
> l'articular del cerebro è perfetto,
> lo motor primo a lui si volge lieto
> sovra tant' arte di natura, e spira
> spirito novo, di vertù repleto,
> che ciò che trova attivo quivi, tira
> in sua sustanzia, e fassi un'alma sola,
> che vive e sente e sé in sé rigira.

Open your heart now to the truth which follows, and be aware that no sooner is the fashioning of the mind complete in the embryo than the first mover turns towards it and, rejoicing in the excellence of nature's handiwork, breathes into it a new spirit complete with its own power, this then drawing into its substance every activity it finds there, making as it does so a single soul that lives, feels, and circles around its own centre.

(*Purgatorio* XXV.67–75)

To be as man, in other words, is to know self not only in the singularity and indeed in the specificity of self, in something approaching a species all of its own (the "adeo ut fere quilibet sua propria specie videatur gaudere" of the *De vulgari eloquentia* at I.iii.1), but in the steady presencing of self to self, and, by way of that steady presencing, in the call to self-actualization, to the shaping of its own historical and eschatological destiny. It is, in short, to know self in the deiformity or God-likeness of self, in its subsisting somewhat after the manner of its maker, of the One who *is* as of the essence.

But with what amounts in this sense to a scarcely less than radiant account of man's coming forth in love from the Godhead as but the first fruits of divine creativity and of his subsisting as a creature empowered to the shaping and substantiation of his own destiny we come to the more properly moral aspect of Dante's meditation hereabouts; for if indeed the miracle that is man in his proper power to deiformity or God-likeness is but the product of a ceaseless opening out of the Godhead in ever fresh channels of love-*creativity*, then by the same token the resolution of this or that instance of specifically human being by the one who says 'I' is but a product of love-*organization*, of a bringing home of every instance of properly human loving along the way to the love given with the act itself of existence. What, then, considered in and for itself, is love?

Love, considered in and for itself, is nothing other, Dante thinks, than that whereby the soul seeks out union with the object of its delight, the key passage here, worth noting both for this and for its sense of the eagerness of it all – of love's hastening to the feast – reading as follows:

Amore, veramente pigliando e sottilmente considerando, non è altro che unimento spirituale de l'anima e de la cosa amata; nel quale unimento di propia sua natura l'anima corre tosto e tardi, secondo che è libera o impedita.

Love, properly and carefully considered, is nothing other than the spiritual union of the soul and the object of its affection, to which union the soul, in keeping with its proper nature, hastens swiftly or slowly according to the degree or otherwise of its freedom.

(*Convivio* III.ii.3)

– lines to which, as confirming both the genesis of love (a matter, this, of the mind's abstracting from the phantasm or raw sensation of seeing a virtual or intentional form thereafter established fast at – as Dante himself puts it at one point – the 'pinnacle of the mind') and the nature of that love as but a matter of inclination or of *tending towards*, we may add this passage from the *Purgatorio*:

L'animo, ch'è creato ad amar presto,
ad ogne cosa è mobile che piace,

tosto che dal piacere in atto è desto.
Vostra apprensiva da esser verace
tragge intenzione, e dentro a voi la spiega,
sì che l'animo ad essa volger face;
e se, rivolto, inver' di lei si piega,
quel piegare è amor, quell'è natura
che per piacer di novo in voi si lega.

The mind, created quick to love, is readily moved towards everything that pleases, as soon as by pleasure it is roused to action. Your perception takes from outward reality an impression and unfolds it within you, so that it makes the mind turn to it; and if the mind, so turned, inclines towards it, that inclination is love, that is nature as bound by pleasure in you afresh.

(*Purgatorio* XVIII.19–27)

But that is only the beginning of it, for, being an intellectual creature in the flesh, man as man loves in any number of different ways, each properly his to enjoy. Man as man, then, loves like the stones beneath his feet in their cleaving to the ground, like the plants high up on the mountainside and in the shady valleys in their need of the sun and the soil, like the beasts of the field in their delighting one in the company of another, and, as a creature of reasonable discerning, as one forever rejoicing in whatsoever things are true, whatsoever things are honest and whatsoever things are just and of good report, the key passage here running as follows:

Onde è da sapere che ciascuna cosa, come detto è di sopra, per la ragione di sopra mostrata ha 'l suo speziale amore. Come le corpora simplici hanno amore naturato in sé a lo luogo proprio, e però la terra sempre discende al centro; lo fuoco ha [amore a] la circunferenza di sopra, lungo lo cielo de la luna, e però sempre sale a quello. Le corpora composte prima, sì come sono le minere, hanno amore a lo luogo dove la loro generazione è ordinata, e in quello crescono e acquistano vigore e potenza; onde vedemo la calamita sempre da la parte de la sua generazione ricevere vertù. Le piante, che sono prima animate, hanno amore a certo luogo più manifestamente, secondo che la complessione richiede; e però vedemo certe piante lungo l'acque quasi c[ontent]arsi, e certe sopra li gioghi de le montagne, e certe ne le piagge e dappiè monti; le quali se si transmutano, o muoiono del tutto o vivono quasi triste, disgiunte dal loro amico. Li animali bruti hanno più manifesto amore non solamente a li luoghi, ma l'uno l'altro vedemo amare. Li uomini hanno loro proprio amore a le perfette e oneste cose. E però che l'uomo, avvegna che una sola sustanza sia, tuttavia [la] forma, per la sua nobilitade, ha in sé e la natura [d'ognuna di] queste cose, tutti questi amori puote avere e tutti li ha.

What, then, we need to understand is this, that, for the reason shown above, everything has its own proper love. Just as simple bodies have within them a natural love for their proper place, which is why earth is always drawn to its centre, and just as fire has a natural love for the sphere above us bordering that of the Moon, and so always rises towards it, so the primary compound bodies, the minerals, have a love for the place where they are created, and where they grow and whence they derive vigour and energy; thus we find that a magnet always acquires its power from the place whence it comes. Plants, which are the primary form of animate being, have a clear preference for certain places, according to their needs; so some plants we see to be at their happiest alongside water, while others thrive on high peaks or else on slopes or in the foothills, all of which either perish or linger on sadly if uprooted and parted from their friends. Brute animals have an even more obvious love, not only for particular places, but for one another. Human beings too have their proper love, in this case for all things good and praiseworthy. And since man, though but one in substance, comprehends by way of the nobility of his form all these things, he can and does love in all these ways.

(*Convivio* III.iii.2–5)

And it is precisely here that the 'love-organization' or 'bringing home' aspect of the argument looms large, and indeed constitutes the very nub of – as Dante understands it – the affective issue in human experience; for given the notion of man's loving quite properly in all these different ways, then within the economy of the whole the lesser stands to be gathered in to the greater as the ground and guarantee of its function as a coefficient of properly human happiness. More exactly, the kind of love engendered by the positive encounter and to which we may therefore say aye or nay (Dante's 'amore d'animo') stands to be brought home to the kind of love all of a piece with existence itself, to the kind of love, that is to say, born of and transparent to the primordial *let it be* of Judeo-Christian sensibility and thereafter the first and final cause of all loving (Dante's 'amore naturale'). In the degree, then, to which the former as but the love generated by the sights and sounds of the world round about is indeed brought home to the latter as but the love coeval and consubstantial with existence itself then all will be well, love in its every aspect facilitating a state of properly human well-being and of properly human happiness. In the degree, by contrast, to which the former remains a law unto itself, free-floating and unaccountable, it subsists merely as a principle of moral and ontological undoing, the soul knowing itself by way only of its apostasy, of – in all the catastrophic substance and consequence thereof – a fresh rising up of the creature against the creator:

> "Né creator né creatura mai",
> cominciò el, "figliuol, fu sanza amore,
> o naturale o d'animo; e tu 'l sai.
>   Lo naturale è sempre sanza errore,
> ma l'altro puote errar per malo obietto
> o per troppo o per poco di vigore.
>   Mentre ch'elli è nel primo ben diretto,
> e ne' secondi sé stesso misura,
> esser non può cagion di mal diletto;
>   ma quando al mal si torce, o con più cura

o con men che non dee corre nel bene,
contra 'l fattore adovra sua fattura".

He began: "neither creator nor creature, my son, was – as
well you know – ever without love, either natural or elective.
Natural love can never err, but the other may err in respect
either of an unworthy object or else by way either of excess
or defect. So long as it is directed on the highest good and as
regards all others is properly proportionate, it cannot be the
cause of doubtful pleasure. But bent upon evil or chasing the
good with more or less zeal than it ought, against the creator
works his creature."

(*Purgatorio* XVII.91–102)

PATTERNS OF SELF-RELATEDNESS: BEING AS *AHEAD* OF SELF, AS *AWAY* FROM SELF AND *ALONGSIDE* SELF

But the argument needs now to be developed in terms of the
patterns of moral and ontological awareness generated by this
situation and present to the more or less anxious subject as the
in-and-through-which of self-understanding; for knowing himself
as he does as a creature of free moral determination and thus of
ultimate accountability, that same more or less anxious subject
knows himself (*a*) as *ahead* of himself in respect of the *what might
be* of his properly human presence in the world; (*b*) as – the call to
orderly self-actualization notwithstanding – *away* from himself on
the plane of willing; and (*c*) as *alongside* himself by way of conscience
as, precisely, a matter of 'with-knowing', of standing critically in one's
own company, these things between them, as present not so much
successively as simultaneously within the complex economy of the
historical instant, making for the twofold agony and ecstasy of it all.

Human being is an order of being *ahead* of itself in that the
individual is forever called to a more consummate presence in the
world on the planes both of knowing and of loving. On the plane
of knowing the call to a more consummate presence in the world
begins with the ordinary business of understanding, where to know

something in respect of its intelligible form is already to be called out of the immediate into the universal, into a sense, that is to say, not merely of the instance but of the class of things generally to which that instance belongs. Turning, then, to the text and touching first on the basic mechanism of understanding, there is the "Vostra apprensiva da esser verace" passage of *Purgatorio* XVIII with its sense of that mechanism as a matter of abstraction, of the mind's eliciting from the raw data or *phantasmata* of perception a mental 'intention' subsequently installed at the – again as Dante himself puts it – pinnacle of the mind as an object of contemplation:

> Vostra apprensiva da esser verace
> tragge intenzione, e dentro a voi la spiega,
> sì che l'animo ad essa volger face;
> e se, rivolto, inver' di lei si piega,
> quel piegare è amor, quell'è natura
> che per piacer di novo in voi si lega.

Your perception takes from outward reality an impression and unfolds it within you, so that it makes the mind turn to it; and if the mind, so turned, inclines thereunto, that inclination is love, that is nature as bound by pleasure in you afresh.

(Purgatorio XVIII.22–27)

– lines to which as constituting an 'eminent' or ultimate statement of understanding thus understood – 'eminent' in the sense of denoting activity at the far limit of cognitive possibility – we may add the 'forma universal' passage of *Paradiso* XXXIII bearing upon the pilgrim poet's lighting at last upon the intelligible form of being in its totality:

> Nel suo profondo vidi che s'interna,
> legato con amore in un volume,
> ciò che per l'universo si squaderna:
> sustanze e accidenti e lor costume
> quasi conflati insieme, per tal modo

che ciò ch'i' dico è un semplice lume.
La forma universal di questo nodo
credo ch'i' vidi, perché più di largo,
dicendo questo, mi sento ch'i' godo.

In its depth I saw that it contained, bound by love in one
volume, that which is scattered in leaves through the universe,
substances and accidents and their relations as it were fused
together in such a way that what I tell of is a simple light.
I think I saw the universal form of this complex, because in
telling it I feel my joy expand.

(*Paradiso* XXXIII.85–93)

But understanding thus understood, as a matter of abstraction,
though it facilitates transcendence on the plane of knowing, is not
the same as that transcendence, for transcendence on the plane of
knowing is a matter of transcending, not the *object*, but the *subject*
of knowing. To speak of transcendence on the plane of knowing as
a property of this or that instance of specifically human being is,
in other words, to speak of the way in which the mind as knowing
is forever engaged at the point of self-reconstruction, of defining
afresh the boundaries of cognitive selfhood. The notion is essential
to a proper understanding of what is going on in the *Paradiso*, for
never in this third canticle of the *Commedia* is it a question simply
of knowing more things or even of knowing some things more fully.
Rather, it is a question of *becoming* on the part of the one who
knows, of the soul's emergence into a new and more ample form of
being-as-understanding. This, at any rate, is Dante's meaning when
in Cantos XXIII and XXX (lines 40–45 and 55–60 respectively) he
speaks of knowing in terms of 'dilation' ("dilatar"), of 'amplification'
("farsi più grande"), of 'issuing forth' ("uscir di sé"), and of
'surmounting' ("sormontar"), terms that confirm his preoccupation
not so much with the known as with the knower:

Come foco di nube si diserra
per dilatarsi sì che non vi cape,

e fuor di sua natura in giù s'atterra,
 la mente mia così, tra quelle dape
fatta più grande, di sé stessa uscìo,
e che si fesse rimembrar non sape.
 ...

 Non fur più tosto dentro a me venute
queste parole brievi, ch'io compresi
me sormontar di sopr' a mia virtute;
 e di novella vista mi raccesi
tale, che nulla luce è tanto mera,
che li occhi miei non si fosser difesi.

As fire breaks from a cloud, swelling till it has not room there, and against its nature falls to the earth, so my mind, made greater at that feast, was transported from itself and of what it became has no remembrance ... No sooner had these brief words reached my mind than I was conscious of rising beyond my own powers, and such new vision was kindled in me that there is no light so bright my eyes would not have borne it.

In neither of these passages is it a question merely of accumulation, of adding more to the stock of understanding, though this too is there in them both; for adding more to the stock of understanding, taken in itself and without reference to the situation of the one who understands, is conducive not to self-finding but to self-losing, to the soul's foundering amid the immensity of it all. To know in keeping with the deepest exigencies of human nature, Dante suggests, is to become ever more powerful in point of knowing, ever more equal to the world there to be known.

And what applies on the plane of knowing applies also on the plane of loving, for here too it is a question less of the *what* than of the *who* of that loving, of love as the in-and-through-which of a more ample humanity on the part of the lover. True, to love, ordinarily, is to love *something*, a notion that Dante is happy to acknowledge; so, for example, *Convivio* III.ii.3 on what love, precisely as such, actually is, namely the "coming together of the soul and the object of its affection" ("Amore, veramente pigliando e sottilmente considerando, non è altro che unimento spirituale de l'anima e de la cosa amata"), or these lines again from the *Convivio* at III.iii.11 on truth and virtue as between them the object of properly human loving: "E per la quinta e ultima natura, cioè vera umana o, meglio dicendo, angelica, cioè razionale, ha l'uomo amore a la veritade e a la vertude" ("By dint of the fifth and final nature – the nature which is truly human or, better still, angelic, that is, rational – man has a love for truth and virtue"), or these from *Purgatorio* XXXI (lines 22–24) on goodness pure and simple as the *non plus ultra* of human desiring:

> Per entro i mie' disiri,
> che ti menavano ad amar lo bene
> di là dal qual non è a che s'aspiri ...

By way of this, your desire for me, you were confirmed in a love of the good beyond which there is nothing further to be longed for ...

or these from *Paradiso* XI (lines 61–63) relative to Francis and his espousal of My Lady Poverty as his one true love:

> e dinanzi a la sua spirital corte
> et coram patre le si fece unito;
> poscia di dì in dì l'amò più forte.

and before his spiritual court *et coram patre* [in the presence of his father] he was joined to her, and thenceforth loved her better every day.

Love, then, like understanding, has an object, something over against itself that it seeks properly to enjoy. And, like understanding, it too has an *ultimate* object, this ultimate object being nothing less than the Godhead itself as but the first and final cause of everything that *is* as both loved and loving; so, for example, *Convivio* III.ii.7, with its emphasis on the individual's desire to strengthen his otherwise passing presence in the world by way of union with the One who *is* as of the essence:

E però che naturalissimo è in Dio volere essere – però che, sì come ne lo allegato libro si legge, 'prima cosa è l'essere, e anzi a quello nulla è' – l'anima umana essere vuole naturalmente con tutto desiderio; e però che 'l suo essere dipende da Dio e per quello si conserva, naturalmente disia e vuole essere a Dio unita per lo suo essere fortificare.

Since, furthermore, what is most natural to God is the will to be (for in the book quoted above we read that 'What comes first is being, prior to which there is nothing'), the human soul likewise wishes naturally and wholeheartedly to be. And since its being depends on God and is sustained by him, it naturally desires and indeed wills to be united with him for the sake of strengthening that being.

or *Convivio* IV.xii.14, with its sense of man's being moved from beforehand to seek out the One in whose image he is fashioned:

... lo sommo desiderio di ciascuna cosa, e prima da la natura dato, è lo ritornare a lo suo principio. E però che Dio è principio de le nostre anime e fattore di quelle simili a sé (sì come è scritto: 'Facciamo l'uomo ad imagine e similitudine nostra'), essa anima massimamente desidera di tornare a quello.

... the highest desire in every being, and the first implanted in it by nature, is the desire to return to its first cause. Since, further, God is the first cause of our souls, and creates them in his own likeness (for as it is written: 'Let us make man in our own image and likeness'), the soul desires first and foremost to return to him.

or *Paradiso* VII.142–44, with its sense of the soul as connaturally enamoured of God as the alpha and omega of all loving:

35

ma vostra vita sanza mezzo spira
la somma beninanza, e la innamora
di sé sì che poi sempre la disira.

but into you life is straightaway in-breathed by the Supreme
Beneficence, which then so enamours it of himself that it
ceaselessly desires him ever after.

But the soul's reaching out for union with God as the 'Supreme
Beneficence', though it facilitates transcendence on the plane of
loving, is not the same as that transcendence, for transcendence on
the plane of loving is a matter of transcending, not the *object*, but
the *subject* of loving. To speak of transcendence as a property of this
or that instance of specifically human being is, in other words, to
speak of the way in which the mind as loving is forever engaged at
the point of self-reconstruction, of defining afresh the boundaries
of affective selfhood. Here again, then, the notion is essential to a
proper understanding of what is going on in the *Paradiso*, for never
in this third canticle of the *Commedia* is it a question of the soul's
seeking out more things until at last it comes into possession of God
as the ultimate object of desire. Rather, it is a question of *becoming*
on the part of the one who loves, of the soul's emergence into a new
and more ample form of being-as-loving. This, at any rate, is Dante's
meaning in passages such as the following from Cantos X and XIV
of the *Paradiso* (lines 82–87 and 49–51 respectively), where his
emphasis falls less on the object in and for itself of desiring than on
the ever greater capacity for loving on the part of the one who loves.
To love in keeping with the deepest exigencies of human nature,
Dante suggests, is to become ever more powerful in point of loving,
ever more equal to the world there to be loved:

E dentro a l'un senti' cominciar: "Quando
lo raggio de la grazia, onde s'accende
verace amore e che poi cresce amando,
multiplicato in te tanto resplende,
che ti conduce su per quella scala

u' sanza risalir nessun discende ..."

...

 onde la visïon crescer convene,
crescer l'ardor che di quella s'accende,
crescer lo raggio che da esso vene.

And within one I heard begin: "Since the beam of grace by which true love is kindled and which then grows by loving shines so multiplied in you that it brings you up that stair which none descends but to mount again" ... from that must vision increase, the ardour increase that is kindled by it, and the radiance increase which comes from that.

Here as throughout this third canticle of the poem, the line has about it a subjective to the point of mystical intensity as the soul prepares to lose itself in God as the principle of all light and love. But rarely in Christian mysticism, and certainly not here in Dante, does self-loss in God exhaust the spiritual undertaking, for the soul's self-losing in God is always and everywhere the way of its self-finding, of – to make use of Paul's ringing terminology as relayed by the Authorized Version – its growing into the 'stature of the fullness' of what it has it in itself to be and to become. To suppose otherwise – to imagine that it is all a question of abandoning self to the other-than-self in a kind of nirvanic forgetfulness – is at once to drain the text of what most matters about it, namely its transparency to the *let it be* there on the threshold of the entire Judeo-Christian undertaking.

This, then, is what it means to speak of being as *ahead* of itself. To speak of being as *ahead* of itself is to speak of self under the aspect of its proper projectedness, of its knowing self, that is to say, by way of the call to an ever more ample humanity on the planes both of knowing and of loving. Never, even in the moment of maximum recalcitrance, can there ever be any question of denying or of disguising what in this sense amounts to a summons equiprimordial with being itself, man, even in the moment of maximum recalcitrance, knowing himself in the ideally if not actually ecstatic substance of his presence in the world.

Human being is an order of being *away* from itself in the
sense of – the call to transcendence notwithstanding – forever
subsisting in the grip of dividedness on the plane of willing, a
situation conveniently approached by way of the tension always and
everywhere verifiable in human experience at the point of transition
between essence and existence, the point at which, sensitive to the
fundamentally ecstatic reasons of his properly human presence in
the world as a free determinant, the individual sets about the task
of historical actualization. *Essentially*, then, man as man knows
himself in, again, the projectedness of his properly human presence
in the world, in terms, that is to say, of the call operative both from
beforehand and from out of the depths *to be* over and beyond self
on the planes of knowing and loving – something that, from a
theological point of view, means *to be* by way of participation in the
One who *is* as the beginning and end of all being. Any number of
passages testify to the strength of Dante's commitment hereabouts,
to his sense of the individual man or woman as caught up before
ever he or she thinks about it in a species of yearning as pressing
as it is persistent; so, for example, in addition to the "naturalmente
disia e vuole essere a Dio unita" and the "essa anima massimamente
desidera di tornare a quello" moment of the *Convivio* cited just
a moment ago, the "appressando sé al suo disire" passage on the
threshold of the *Paradiso*:

> Nel ciel che più de la sua luce prende
> fu' io, e vidi cose che ridire
> né sa né può chi di là sù discende;
> perché appressando sé al suo disire,
> nostro intelletto si profonda tanto,
> che dietro la memoria non può ire.

I was in the heaven that most receives his light and saw things
which he that comes therefrom has neither the knowledge nor
the power to tell again; for our intellect, drawing near to its
desire, sinks so deep that memory cannot follow in its wake.

(*Paradiso* I.4–9)

or the "ardor del desiderio in me finii" passage no less prominent in
its final phase:

> E io ch'al fine di tutt' i disii
> appropinquava, sì com' io dovea,
> l'ardor del desiderio in me finii.

And I, approaching as I was the object of my yearning, knew
quite properly the stilling of my every desire.

(Paradiso XXXIII.46–48)

Throughout, then, it is a question of man as antecedently aware, as
knowing and interpreting himself in terms of an end or objective
coeval and consubstantial with his very *being there* in the world,
an end or objective thus predating the moral moment proper of
human experience – the moment, that is to say, of deciding one way
or another – and, ideally at least, serving either to countenance or
to constrain each successive movement of the spirit.

Existentially, by contrast, or at the point of transition between
reason and reality the individual knows himself not so much in the
directedness as in the *distractedness* of self, in his readiness despite
every inclination to the contrary to espouse the alternative project,
the surrogate or stand-in scheme apt to deliver him to something
closer to nothingness than to somethingness on the plane of properly
human being. This at any rate is where Dante begins his own Dasein
analytic in the *Commedia*, his own account of the *how it is and how
it fares* with this or that individual (Heidegger's 'wie einem ist und
wird') under the conditions of time and space. More than ordinarily
sensitive now to the tragic substance of specifically human being in
its moment-by-moment implementation, he begins at the point of
dividedness on the plane of willing, of the fear of radical self-losing, of
the slumberousness and inexplicability of it all, and, as the boundary
condition of these things, of despair as but the encompassing:

> Nel mezzo del cammin di nostra vita
> mi ritrovai per una selva oscura,

ché la diritta via era smarrita.
   Ahi quanto a dir qual era è cosa dura
esta selva selvaggia e aspra e forte
che nel pensier rinova la paura!
   Tant' è amara che poco è più morte;
ma per trattar del ben ch'i' vi trovai,
dirò de l'altre cose ch'i' v'ho scorte.
   Io non so ben ridir com' i' v'intrai,
tant' era pien di sonno a quel punto
che la verace via abbandonai.
   ...

   Poi ch'èi posato un poco il corpo lasso,
ripresi via per la piaggia diserta,
sì che 'l piè fermo sempre era 'l più basso.
   Ed ecco, quasi al cominciar de l'erta,
una lonza leggera e presta molto,
che di pel macolato era coverta;
   e non mi si partia dinanzi al volto,
anzi 'mpediva tanto il mio cammino,
ch'i' fui per ritornar più volte vòlto.
   ...

   Ed una lupa, che di tutte brame
sembiava carca ne la sua magrezza,
e molte genti fé già viver grame,
   questa mi porse tanto di gravezza
con la paura ch'uscia di sua vista,
ch'io perdei la speranza de l'altezza.

In the middle of the journey of our life I came to myself
within a dark wood where the straight way was lost. Ah, how
hard a thing it is to tell of that wood, savage, harsh and dense,
the very thought of which renews my fear. So bitter is it that
death is hardly more. But to give an account of the good I
found in that place I shall tell of the other things I discovered
there. I cannot rightly say how I came to be there, so full of
sleep was I when I left the true path ... After I had rested

my weary frame a little I set out again over the desert slope;
and lo, just about at the beginning of that slope, there before
me was a leopard light and swift, its hide everywhere spotted,
and neither did it go from before my face but so impeded my
way that many a time I turned to go back ... and a she-wolf
which – having brought many a man to destitution – seemed
in its leanness to be charged with all craving. This last weighed
so heavily upon me by way of the terror it emanated that I lost
hope of any ascent.

(Inferno I.1–12, 28–36 and 49–54)

Why this should be so – why the soul alert if only hazily to the *what
might be* of its presence in the world as a creature in potential to the
most radical kind of transcendence on the planes of knowing and
loving should in the event opt in a moment of self-apostasy for the
alternative project – is indeed the great imponderable, even Dante's
account of it in terms of perverse loving scarcely reaching down
that far. *That* it is so, however, is confirmed by the agony of it all, by
the admixture of fear and fortitude, of resignation and resolve, and
of hope and hopelessness as in the midst of this life of ours the soul
commits itself withal to the business of ontological undoing.

This, then, is what it means to speak of the *awayness* of this or
that instance of specifically human being in its positive unfolding.
To speak of the *awayness* of this or that instance of specifically
human being in its positive unfolding is to speak of a co-presencing
at the centre of that being of the *will to be* and the *will not to be* apt
in the absence of contrition as but a bruising or breaking down of
the old in favour of the new to bring the soul to the brink of despair,
at which point the tension always and everywhere verifiable in the
recesses of self between the divine and the demonic moves fully and
unequivocally into view.

Human being is an order of being *alongside* itself in the sense
that, called from beforehand to the most radical kind of self-
surpassing on the planes both of knowing and of loving and yet
ceaselessly waylaid by the alternative project, it is forever present

to itself as a matter of concern – a situation usefully approached by way (*a*) of guilt as the sensation of dividedness on the plane of properly human being, and (*b*) of the at once classical and Christian-theological notion of conscience as a matter of *self-with-knowing*, of self-awareness as the whereabouts of awareness generally.

Guilt as the sensation of dividedness on the plane of specifically human being is present to the individual under two aspects: the shared guilt of the Fall and the guilt incurred by the individual in the moment of self-delivery, in the making over of self despite self to the self-consciously inauthentic project, the latter being but a discrete manifestation of the former as but its deep and abiding substance. As far, then, as the shared guilt of the Fall is concerned, Dante, in the course of a soteriology as careful as it is courageous, offers an account both of its reason and of its remedy. Adam, he says, in injuring himself, injured his whole progeny, which from that point on lay in its infirmity until the expiatory work of Christ made possible a fresh reconciliation between man and God:

> Per non soffrire a la virtù che vole
> freno a suo prode, quell'uom che non nacque,
> dannando sé, dannò tutta sua prole;
>   onde l'umana specie inferma giacque
> giù per secoli molti in grande errore,
> fin ch'al Verbo di Dio discender piacque
>   u' la natura, che dal suo fattore
> s'era allungata, unì a sé in persona
> con l'atto sol del suo etterno amore.

By not enduring for his good a rein upon his will, the man that was never born, condemning himself, condemned all his progeny; therefore mankind lay sick below in great error for many ages, till it pleased the Word of God, which, coming among us and by the sole act of its eternal love, assumed in its own person the nature that had thus forsaken its maker.

(*Paradiso* VII.25–33)

This, he goes on, was deemed by God to be the only way of saving the situation, for, try as he might, man in his own strength was incapable of rising to the extent that he had fallen. Only by way, therefore, of Christ's living and dying as man for man might justice be done, this living and dying as man for man, however, serving within the love-economy of the whole to confirm man's status as, in some sense and in some degree, party to his own resurrection:

> Ficca mo l'occhio per entro l'abisso
> de l'etterno consiglio, quanto puoi
> al mio parlar distrettamente fisso.
> Non potea l'uomo ne' termini suoi
> mai sodisfar, per non potere ir giuso
> con umiltate obedïendo poi,
> quanto disobediendo intese ir suso;
> e questa è la cagion per che l'uom fue
> da poter sodisfar per sé dischiuso.
> Dunque a Dio convenia con le vie sue
> riparar l'omo a sua intera vita,
> dico con l'una, o ver con amendue.
> Ma perché l'ovra tanto è più gradita
> da l'operante, quanto più appresenta
> de la bontà del core ond'ell'è uscita,
> la divina bontà che 'l mondo imprenta,
> di proceder per tutte le sue vie,
> a rilevarvi suso, fu contenta.
> Né tra l'ultima notte e 'l primo die
> sì alto o sì magnifico processo,
> o per l'una o per l'altra, fu o fie:
> ché più largo fu Dio a dar sé stesso
> per far l'uom sufficiente a rilevarsi,
> che s'elli avesse sol da sé dimesso;
> e tutti li altri modi erano scarsi
> a la giustizia, se 'l Figliuol di Dio
> non fosse umiliato ad incarnarsi.

Fix your eyes now within the abyss of the eternal counsel and give your closest heed to my words. Man could never, within his limits, give satisfaction, for he could not go so low in humility, by subsequent obedience, as, by disobedience, he had thought to go high; and this is the cause whereby man was debarred from the power of giving satisfaction by himself. It was needful, therefore, that by his own ways God should restore man to his full life – by one way, that is, or by both. But since the deed gratifies the doer more the more it manifests of the goodness of the heart from which it springs, the divine goodness that puts its imprint on the world was pleased to proceed by all its ways to raise you up again; nor between the last night and the first day was there or will there be a procedure by the one way or the other so lofty or so glorious. For with a view to enabling man in respect of his own raising up God was more bounteous in giving himself than if, simply of himself, he had pardoned him; and all other means came short of justice save that the Son of God should humble himself to become flesh.

(*Paradiso* VII.94–120)

A soteriology or theology of salvation, then, indeed as careful as it is courageous, since for all its sense of the indispensability of the divine initiative hereabouts, of God's having of necessity to step in afresh for the purposes of making good man's first disobedience, this is a soteriology apt even so to honour the human project, this precisely – this co-involvement of man at the point of his raising up – being what it means to speak of "maturity in the flame of love", of letting a thing be in the fullness of that being:

> Tu dici: "Ben discerno ciò ch'i' odo;
> ma perché Dio volesse, m'è occulto,
> a nostra redenzion pur questo modo".
> Questo decreto, frate, sta sepulto
> a li occhi di ciascuno il cui ingegno
> ne la fiamma d'amor non è adulto.

You say: "I discern clearly what I hear; but for me darkling still is why God should have chosen this means of our redemption." This decree, brother, lies buried from the eyes of each and every one of those spirits less than adult in the flame of love.

(*Paradiso* VII.55–60)

Usually, however, when Dante uses the terminology of guilt ('colpa', 'rio', 'reo', 'difetto', etc.) he is thinking, not of the shared guilt of the Fall, but of the actual guilt incurred by the individual, of the guilt engendered by the delivery of self to something other, and something less, than a properly human presence in the world; so, for example, the "per la dannosa colpa de la gola" ("for the ruinous fault of gluttony") of *Inferno* VI.53 or the "diverse colpe giù li grava al fondo" ("different faults weigh them down to the depths") of VI.86 or the "quando la colpa pentuta è rimossa" ("when their repented guilt is removed") of XIV.138, where the term 'colpa' has about it the sense not of inherited but of actual guilt, of private commission or omission. But – and this now is the point – whether we are thinking of the inherited guilt of original sin or of the incurred guilt of actual sin, guilt is always a matter of ontological concern, for guilt, properly understood, is nothing other than the felt-sensation of being in its dividedness, that whereby the individual knows self in the alienation of self. Once acknowledged and received into self as the first step towards its liquidation, guilt thus understood is drained of its power to destroy, herein, in its emasculation as a principle of undoing, lying the beginning of new life – the substance, precisely, of the Dantean *Purgatorio*. Left to itself, however, it persists to tax the individual with the fractured character of his existence and to confirm him in a sense of the *minus esse* or diminished stature of his presence in the world as a free determinant – the substance, precisely, of the Dantean *Inferno*.

The notion of conscience as a matter of *with knowing* or as standing critically in one's own company goes back a long way. Thus Socrates among the ancients speaks of an inner voice or *daemon* calling the individual to account, while Cicero speaks of wickedness as but a burden on *conscientia*, the turning back of self upon self in a spirit of misgiving thus already figuring as a structure of properly human awareness. It is only later, however, in the context of a now secure sense of man's fall from grace, that the idea is subject to systematic development. The chief distinction here is between synderesis and conscience proper. On the one hand, then, and tending at first to prevail over the notion of conscience as a matter of *with knowing* pure and simple, there is that of synderesis as denoting something approaching a connatural sense of righteousness, a 'scintilla rationis' or 'spark of reason' that even in the most depraved of spirits cannot be extinguished; so, for example, Thomas with his sense in the *Summa theologiae* (Ia IIae.94.1 ad 2) of synderesis as but the "natural law of our mind" ("synderesis dicitur lex intellectus nostri"), a set of first principles given with the act itself of existence. Not so, however, for Dante, conscience for him consisting of something closer to *remorse* as a 'biting back' of self in circumstances of bad faith or of doubtful intention. True, some passages suggest a more kindly presence, conscience in the case, for example, of *Inferno* XV serving merely to guarantee the honest utterance, the truth of what the pilgrim poet now has it in mind to say:

> Tanto vogl'io che vi sia manifesto,
> pur che mia coscïenza non mi garra,
> ch' a la Fortuna, come vuol, son presto.

This much I would have you understand clearly, that, provided my conscience does not chide me, I am ready for Fortune whatsoever she wills.

(*Inferno* XV.91–93)

– lines to which we might add these from Canto XXVIII on conscience as a good companion, as but the breastplate of truth and of truthfulness:

> Ma io rimasi a riguardar lo stuolo,
> e vidi cosa ch'io avrei paura,

sanza più prova, di contarla solo;
  se non che coscïenza m'assicura,
la buona compagnia che l'uom francheggia
sotto l'asbergo del sentirsi pura.

But I stayed to watch the troop and saw a thing I should fear
even to mention without more proof, but that conscience as
but the good companion that emboldens a man under the
breastplate of his feeling himself whole reassures me.

(*Inferno* XXVIII.112–17)

But companionship aside, it is the *remorse* or 'biting back' component
of the argument that most vigorously engages Dante's attention,
several passages serving to confirm the notion of conscience as but
a squaring up of self to self in the innermost parts thereof; so, for
example, these lines from Canto XIX of the *Inferno* bearing in the
case of the simonists or traders in ecclesiastical office upon the prick
of conscience, upon its power in circumstances of contritionlessness
to convulse mind and body alike:

E mentr' io li cantava cotai note,
  o ira o cosciïenza che 'l mordesse,
forte spingava con ambo le piote.

And as to him I sang this song, whether bitten by anger or by
conscience he kicked out hard with both feet.

(*Inferno* XIX.118–20)

or, with reference to Virgil as no less than Dante himself caught up
by the beauty of Casella's singing on the shores of the mountain,
these from *Purgatorio* III on conscience and distractedness, on a
lingering of the spirit on the plane of the aesthetic:

El mi parea da sé stesso rimorso:
  o dignitosa cosciïenza e netta,
come t'è picciol fallo amaro morso!

47

He seemed to me smitten with self-reproach. O pure and noble conscience, how bitter a sting to you is a little fault!

(*Purgatorio* III.7–9)

or these from the other end of the canticle on Dante's struggle to recall the when, where and why of his alienation from Beatrice in the wake of her demise:

> Non mi ricorda
> ch'i' stranïasse me già mai da voi,
> né honne coscïenza che rimorda.

I have no remembrance that I ever strayed from you, nor have I conscience of it that pricks me.

(*Purgatorio* XXXIII.91–93)

In each of these cases, then, conscience functions as a principle of self-confrontation, as that whereby the individual is summoned into his or her own presence as a creature both of accountability and – more especially – of self-accountability, of self-presencing on the plane of properly human being. This, emphatically, does not imply contrition in the brokenness thereof; for contrition in the brokenness thereof, though it presupposes the biting-back of conscience thus understood, constitutes a further and distinctive movement of the spirit, namely a taking into self of the guilt of self as the first step towards its liquidation. Conscience, in other words, as but a biting-back of self in the innermost parts of self subsists merely on the threshold of something still greater than itself, to wit of repentance as a matter of soul-sorrowing, of Bernard's 'assiduitas lacrymarum' or abundance of tears.

But with this we are still on the lower slopes where Dante and conscience are concerned, for conscience in Dante is subject to contemplation not so much in and for itself as by way of the strategies invoked in circumstances of contritionlessness for the purposes of holding it at bay. For in circumstances of contritionlessness – and here we come close to the still centre of Dante's meditation in the *Inferno*, of the pathology as he understands it of radical self-alienation – there can be no standing securely in one's own presence, indeed no standing at all, short of one or other of the means of self-preservation, of either *frantic self-exoneration* or *loud proclamation* as a way of stilling the forever unquiet voice of conscience as *with-knowing*.

To take first, then, the case of *frantic self-exoneration*, this is everywhere discernible in the *Inferno* as, whatever else it is, an account of the soul's *awayness* from self in point of fundamental willing, of its standing more or less systematically over against the synderectic substance of its properly human presence in the world. Sensitive to the *what might be* of that same presence in the world as a creature of reasonable moral determination, but impressed by the depth of its self-betrayal and by this as a principle of ontic annihilation, of the shading off of somethingness into nothingness on the plane of properly human being, it has no alternative but to shift the burden of guilt, to implicate an often enough mythological third party; so, for example, Francesca – the scarcely less than gracious Francesca – among the adulterous in Canto V of the *Inferno* with her indictment of Amore as the beginning and end of her woe:

> "Amor, ch'al cor gentil ratto s'apprende,
> prese costui de la bella persona
> che mi fu tolta; e 'l modo ancor m'offende.
> Amor, ch'a nullo amato amar perdona,
> mi prese del costui piacer sì forte,
> che, come vedi, ancor non m'abbandona.
> Amor condusse noi ad una morte.
> Caina attende chi a vita ci spense".
> Queste parole da lor ci fuor porte.

"Love, which is quickly kindled in the noble heart, seized this man for the fair form that was taken from me, and the manner afflicts me still. Love, which absolves no one from loving, seized me so strongly with his charm that, as you see, it does not leave me yet. Love brought us to one death. Caina waits for him who quenched our life."These words were borne from them to us.

(*Inferno* V.100–108)

or Pier delle Vigne among the violent against self in Canto XIII with his putting it all down to the harlot jealousy as the guilty party:

La meretrice che mai da l'ospizio
di Cesare non torse li occhi putti,
morte comune e de le corti vizio,
   infiammò contra me li animi tutti;
e li 'nfiammati infiammar sì Augusto,
che 'lieti onor tornaro in tristi lutti.
   L'animo mio, per disdegnoso gusto,
credendo col morir fuggir disdegno,
ingiusto fece me contra me giusto.

The harlot that never turned her eyes from Caesar's household, the common bane and the vice of our courts, inflamed all minds against me, and those inflamed so inflamed Augustus that happy honours turned to dismal woes. My mind, in scornful temper thinking by dying to escape from scorn, made me unjust to my just self.

(*Inferno* XIII.64–72)

or Guido da Montefeltro among the false counsellors in Canto XXVII with his indictment of the 'great priest' Boniface VIII no less as the cause of his undoing:

S'i' credesse che mia risposta fosse
a persona che mai tornasse al mondo,
questa fiamma staria sanza più scosse;
   ma però che già mai di questo fondo

non tornò vivo alcun, s'i' odo il vero,
sanza tema d'infamia ti rispondo.
  Io fui uom d'arme, e poi fui cordigliero,
credendomi, sì cinto, fare ammenda;
e certo il creder mio venìa intero,
  se non fosse il gran prete, a cui mal prenda!,
che mi rimise ne le prime colpe;
e come e quare, voglio che m'intenda.

If I thought my answer were to one who would ever return to the world, this flame should stay without another flinch; but since – if what I hear is true – none ever returned alive from this depth I make reply without fear of infamy. I was a man of arms and then a corded friar, thinking, so girt, to make amends; and indeed my trust hereabouts would have borne fruit but for the great priest – may ill befall him – who put me back in my old sins, and the how and why of it I would have you hear from me.

(Inferno XXVII.61–72)

In all these cases, as indeed whenever the soul in want of contrition has recourse to *frantic self-exoneration* as a means of coping with self in circumstances of self-delivery, the strategy is both ironic and duplicitous: ironic in that, far from easing the sensation of guilt, it merely reinforces it, strengthening beyond words the soul's sense of standing now in the grip of despair as the boundary condition of being in its estrangement, and duplicitous in that, as but a strategy or surface mechanism of assuagement, it leaves the soul free to live out again – and again and again – the substance of its self-consciously disordered existence. But for all its serving by way of irony and disingenuousness to compound the spirit's sense of suffering it is indispensable, for short of the disclaimer, the soul in its far-offness is forever confronted by the anomaly at the heart of its presence in the world as a free determinant, the anomaly implicit in its delivering itself despite itself to the self-consciously surrogate scheme. Short of the disclaimer, it is forever at the mercy of its own biting back, of the unkind presence of self to self as self-knowing.

Likewise prominent as a means of sidestepping the anomaly of it all in circumstances of contritionlessness is the kind of *loud proclamation* whereby, confronted in conscience by the gravity of its self-betrayal, the spirit resorts to a still more forceful proclamation of the leading project, forcefulness, in circumstances of contritionlessness, being not without a persuasiveness of its own; so, for example, among the heretics but notable above all for his particular brand of political partisanship, Farinata, troubled, to be sure, by an uncomfortable sense of his own disruptiveness in the world (the "quella nobil patrïa natio, / a la qual forse fui troppo molesto" of *Inferno* X.26–27) but nonetheless given over to a massive and massively insistent reiteration of a now inveterate habit of mind (the "Chi fuor li maggior tui", or "Who were your ancestors?" of line 42 now bellowed vacuously into all eternity):

> Ed el mi disse: "Volgiti! Che fai?
> Vedi là Farinata che s'è dritto:
> da la cintola in sù tutto 'l vedrai".
> Io avea già il mio viso nel suo fitto;
> ed el s'ergea col petto e con la fronte
> com' avesse l'inferno a gran dispitto.
> E l'animose man del duca e pronte
> mi pinser tra le sepulture a lui,
> dicendo: "Le parole tue sien conte".
> Com' io al piè de la sua tomba fui,
> guardommi un poco, e poi, quasi sdegnoso,
> mi dimandò: "Chi fuor li maggior tui?".

And he said to me: "Turn around. What ails thee? See there Farinata who has risen up erect; from the middle up you will see him there in his full stature." My eyes were already fixed on his and he straightened himself in breast and brow as though holding all hell in scorn, and the bold and ready hands of my leader pushed me between the tombs toward him, saying

the while: "Choose carefully your words." Once I was at the
foot of his tomb he looked at me a little, and then, as though
disdainfully, enquired of me: "Who were your ancestors?"

(*Inferno* X.31–42)

or, as a further instance of commitment come what may to the
leading idea, the case of Ulysses among the false counsellors,
likewise troubled by a sense of the foolishness of it all (the "folle
volo" or "foolish flight" moment of XXVI.125), but likewise loud in
its commendation:

> "O frati", dissi "che per cento milia
> perigli siete giunti a l'occidente,
> a questa tanto picciola vigilia
>   d'i nostri sensi ch'è del rimanente,
> non vogliate negar l'esperïenza,
> di retro al sol, del mondo sanza gente.
>   Considerate la vostra semenza:
> fatti non foste a viver come bruti,
> ma per seguir virtute e canoscenza".

"O brothers," I said, "who through a hundred thousand perils
have reached the west, to this so brief vigil of the senses that
remains to us choose not to deny experience, in the sun's track,
of the unpeopled world. Take thought of the seed from which
you spring. You were not born to live as brutes but to follow
virtue and knowledge."

(*Inferno* XXVI.112–20)

Each of these strategies, as its practitioner knows full well, is
no more than that – a device designed to stave off as far as may
be the trauma of despair and of immanent and indeed of actual
nothingness on the plane of properly human being. But for all its
self-conscious fragility, its hopeless inadequacy to the business in
hand, it must be maintained, for to renounce the strategy is at once

to deliver self to the contradiction at the centre of historical being and to the catastrophe of which contradiction is the nub.

This, then, is what it means to speak of the *alongsidedness* of specifically human being in its moment-by-moment unfolding. To speak of the *alongsidedness* of specifically human being in its moment-by-moment unfolding is to speak (*a*) of conscience as but a murmuring-back of the spirit in the name and for the sake of the twofold integrity and intelligibility of the one who says 'I', and (*b*) of the ways and means of softening and indeed of silencing that same murmuring-back of the spirit in circumstances of perverse loving, of the self-consciously inauthentic project. Thus understood – as the mechanism of man's proper self-presencing as man – conscience functions as a principle both of the ecstasy and of the agony of it all, both of the deiformity to which he is called from out of the depths and of the despair to which, the call to deiformity notwithstanding, he fully and freely delivers himself.

A PHENOMENOLOGY OF BEING

With this – with what in Dante amounts to an account of self and of selfhood in terms (*a*) of the coming about of the rational soul as an immediate product of divine creativity and (*b*) of the geometry of specifically human being in its moment-by-moment unfolding, of its being *ahead* of itself by way of its projectedness on the planes both of knowing and of loving, its being *away* from itself by way of its dividedness in point of willing, and its being *alongside* itself by way of conscience as but a murmuring-back of self from out of the depths – we come finally to the phenomenological aspect of the matter, to the notion everywhere decisive for Dante's procedure in the *Commedia* of the *mood* of being as everywhere transparent to the *truth* of being, to the shape and substance of the already in-abiding ἔσχατος. Already, then, on the threshold of the *Inferno* it is a question of fear, of the kind of fear engendered not now by the occasional occurrence but by being itself as astray in respect of its own innermost reasons, as ranged over against itself at the point of fundamental willing:

54

Nel mezzo del cammin di nostra vita
mi ritrovai per una selva oscura,
ché la diritta via era smarrita.
Ahi quanto a dir qual era è cosa dura
esta selva selvaggia e aspra e forte
che nel pensier rinova la paura!
Tant'è amara che poco è più morte;
ma per trattar del ben ch'i' vi trovai,
dirò de l'altre cose ch'i' v'ho scorte.
Io non so ben ridir com'i' v'intrai,
tant'era pien di sonno a quel punto
che la verace via abbandonai.

Midway in the journey of our life I found myself in a dark wood, for the straight way was lost. Try as I may, there is no telling how it was with that wood, so wild, rugged and harsh was it that even to think of it terrifies me afresh! So savage, in fact, that death itself is scarcely more. But for the sake of the good I found there, I'll tell of what else I saw. How I came to be there I cannot rightly say, so drowsy was I in the moment I forsook the true way.

(*Inferno* I.1–12)

It is, then, by way of fear thus understood, as the rhythm of ontic anxiety, that the individual is alerted to and confirmed in a sense of his imminent demise (the "che poco è più morte" of line 7) as a creature of significant self-determination.

But that is only the beginning, for knowing himself as he does in his far-wandering, he knows himself too in the anger, in the restlessness and, as the whereabouts both of these and of every other indisposition of the spirit, in the despair generated by and indeed all of a piece with a now settled sense of the exitlessness of it all, of there being nothing for it but an indefinite commitment to the self-consciously inauthentic project; so, for example, on the anger aroused by that same self-consciously inauthentic project but – as is the way of it in hell – visited upon every circumstance of the individual's existence, these lines from early on in the text:

> Bestemmiavano Dio e lor parenti,
> l'umana spezie e 'l luogo e 'l tempo e 'l seme
> di lor semenza e di lor nascimenti.

They blasphemed God, their parents and mankind as a whole, together with the place, the time and the seed of their begetting and birth.

(Inferno III.103–105)

while in respect of the restlessness of being in its far-wandering, of the drivenness whereby the soul busies itself about one proximate possibility after another, the "I would never have thought that death had undone so many" moment of a little earlier in the same canto, the canto of those who, living on somewhere between indolence and indifference, knew neither praise nor blame:

> E io, che riguardai, vidi una 'nsegna
> che girando correva tanto ratta,
> che d'ogne posa mi parea indegna;
> e dietro le venìa sì lunga tratta
> di gente, ch'i' non averei creduto
> che morte tanta n'avesse disfatta.

And I, looking on, saw a banner, which, whirling as it went, raced on so swiftly that it seemed to me impatient of any pause, and behind it came so long a train of folk that I would never have believed death had undone so many.

(Inferno III.52–57)

But prominent as they are in this first canticle of the *Commedia*, fear, anger and restlessness thus understood are each of them referable to despair as the encompassing, as the root and abiding condition of every dis-ease of the spirit in circumstances of inauthentic being – the imperative writ large over hell's gate (the "Abandon all hope you that enter here" of *Inferno* III.9) shading off in this sense into the indicative as the still centre of Dante's existential analytic in the *Inferno*. Despair as the root condition of human being in its estrangement is a matter of concern among both the ancients and the moderns. Among the ancients, Augustine, Rabanus Maurus, Richard of St Victor and Bernard of Clairvaux all seek to analyse its psychological structure and to confirm its status as a principle of ontological denial. Augustine, in the *Confessions*, underlines the element of despair at work in obduracy and obsession, its nature as existential listlessness, and the function of faith (in the sense of confidence in the recreative purposes of God) as its polar counterpart. Rabanus Maurus, in the *De videndo Deum*, speaks of it as a matter of spiritual incapacitation, while Richard of St Victor traces it back to ontological fear and Bernard of Clairvaux stresses its nature as spiritual forgetfulness. Among the moderns, Kierkegaard speaks of despair as the mood of the soul's self-unrelatedness, while Tillich speaks of it as a product of conflict in the recesses of personality. Each of these emphases is present in Dante, whose *Inferno*, variously to the point of infinitely nuanced as it is when it comes to the psychopathology of far-wandering, reflects them each and every one in its moment-by-moment verification. But in Dante there is more besides, for despair, in Dante, is a matter not merely of renunciation in the face of adversity, but of the demonic, of a delivery of self to the ways and means of ontic annihilation, of, in short, standing foursquare over and against the primordial *let it be*. Thus Francesca's commitment to the old dance, articulated as it is with exemplary grace and courtesy, contains within itself a gesture of defiance no less absolute than that, say, of Vanni Fucci or Capaneo. And the plaintiveness of Pier delle Vigne, everywhere designed to justify his unjust self, contains within it an effrontery as grave as anything on the lips or in the heart of, say, Filippo Argenti or Bocca degli Alberti among the wrathful and the treacherous respectively. And what applies to Francesca and Pier delle Vigne applies too, for all their magnanimity, to Farinata, Brunetto Latini, Ulysses and

Ugolino; for magnanimity, in circumstances of contritionlessness, is never innocent of impiety, of, withal, the will to destruction.

Provided only, then, that we locate every secondary symptom of unlikeness – of the soul's living on in a 'regio dissimilitudinis' – within the context of despair as but a constant making over of self to the self-consciously impossible project, we have a psychology of self-losing as powerful and as persuasive as anything in European letters. And what applies in the area of self-losing applies too in the area of self-finding, of the soul's coming home to the fullness of its proper humanity. First, then, there is the peace whereby, having trodden the upward way, the purgatorial way of sorrowing and striving, the soul rejoices at last in the perfect stability and self-possession of its properly human presence in the world. With its every love-impulse now harvested, it delights in the 'wholeness' of its being (the "oh vita integra d'amore e di pace!" of the Petrine canto *par excellence* of the *Commedia*, *Paradiso* XXVII), in, as Bernard of Clairvaux puts it, the 'supreme tranquillity, the most placid serenity' of the spirit in its drawing nigh; so, for example, in respect of peace as but the stilling of every proper yearning in human experience, this from the *Convivio* at III.vi.7:

Dove è da sapere che ciascuna cosa massimamente desidera la sua perfezione, e in quella si queta ogni suo desiderio.

It is, then, to be understood that what everything seeks out is its own perfection, at which point its every desire is stilled.

or these from the *Purgatorio* at XXVII.115–17:

Quel dolce pome che per tanti rami
cercando va la cura de' mortali,
oggi porrà in pace le tue fami'.

That sweet fruit which the care of mortals goes seeking on so many boughs shall today give peace to your cravings.

while in respect of the peace of settled understanding, these lines from the *Paradiso* at XXX.100–102:

> Lume è là sù che visibile face
> lo creatore a quella creatura
> che solo in lui vedere ha la sua pace.

Light there is above which makes the creator visible to the creature whose only peace lies in seeing him.

or these from the *Paradiso* at XXXI.109–11:

> tal era io mirando la vivace
> carità di colui che 'n questo mondo,
> contemplando, gustò di quella pace.

such was I, gazing on the living charity of him who in this world tasted by way of contemplation that peace.

In each of these cases, peace is the peace of ultimate affirmation. It is the peace contingent upon the soul's embracing and enacting the deep reasons of its properly human presence in the world, upon its standing at last securely in its own company. Peace, in short, is but the mood of being in the stillness thereof. It is but the *static* mood of being in its authenticity.

Joy, by contrast, as all one with peace thus understood within the now gracious economy of the whole, is that whereby the spirit rejoices in the exhilaration of it all, in, as Dante understands it, the self-overflowing of being in its actuality; so for example, on the bliss of self as freed now for a more ample species of knowing and loving, the "more than myself" and the "streams of rejoicing" moment of Canto XVI:

> Io cominciai: "Voi siete il padre mio;
> voi mi date a parlar tutta baldezza;
> voi mi levate sì, ch'i' son più ch'io.
> Per tanti rivi s'empie d'allegrezza

la mente mia, che di sé fa letizia
perché può sostener che non si spezza".

I began: "You are my father, you give me all boldness to speak,
you uplift me so that I am more than myself; by so many
streams my mind is filled with happiness that it rejoices in
itself yet without fear of bursting."

(*Paradiso* XVI.16–21)

or on the joy of coming home at last on the plane of being-as-
existence, the "but now you are so close" moment of Canto XXII:

"Tu se' sì presso a l'ultima salute",
cominciò Beatrice, "che tu dei
aver le luci tue chiare e acute;
  e però, prima che tu più t'inlei,
rimira in giù, e vedi quanto mondo
sotto li piedi già esser ti fei;
  sì che 'l tuo cor, quantunque può, giocondo
s'appresenti a la turba trïunfante
che lieta vien per questo etera tondo".

"You are so near to the final blessedness," Beatrice began, "that
you must have your eyes clear and keen; and therefore, before
you go further into it, look down and see how much of the
universe I have already put beneath your feet, so that with all
fullness of joy your heart may present itself to the triumphal
host that comes rejoicing through this rounded ether."

(*Paradiso* XXII.124–32)

or on the rapt sensation of intoning with choirs upon high a fervent
ascription of praise these lines from, again, Canto XXVII:

"Al Padre, al Figlio, a lo Spirito Santo",
cominciò, 'gloria!', tutto 'l paradiso,
sì che m'inebrïava il dolce canto.

Ciò ch'io vedeva mi sembiava un riso
de l'universo; per che mia ebbrezza
intrava per l'udire e per lo viso.
 Oh gioia! oh ineffabile allegrezza!
oh vita intègra d'amore e di pace!
oh sanza brama sicura ricchezza!

"Glory be to the Father and to the Son and to the Holy
Ghost!" all paradise began such that with its sweet song my
spirit reeled. What I saw seemed to be a smile of the universe,
my inebriation being that at once of sight and sound. Oh joy
beyond compare! Oh gladness unutterable! Oh life entire in
love and peace! Oh wealth secure beyond all craving!

(*Paradiso* XXVII.1–9)

or, over against the rapt moment of Canto XXVII – though in truth
all of a piece with it in point both of substance and of significance –
the ne'er so exquisite "sweet distillation" moment of Canto XXXIII:

Da quinci innanzi il mio veder fu maggio
che 'l parlar mostra, ch'a tal vista cede,
e cede la memoria a tanto oltraggio.
 Qual è colüi che sognando vede,
che dopo 'l sogno la passione impressa
rimane, e l'altro a la mente non riede,
 cotal son io, ché quasi tutta cessa
mia visïone, e ancor mi distilla
nel core il dolce che nacque da essa.

From that moment my vision was greater than our speech,
which fails at such a sight, and memory too fails at such excess.
Like him that sees in a dream and after the dream the passion
wrought by it remains and the rest returns not to his mind,
such am I; for my vision almost wholly fades and still there
drops within my heart the sweetness that was born of it.

(*Paradiso* XXXIII.55–63)

Throughout, then, the pattern is the same, joy in its pure form being, for Dante, the joy contingent on the soul's coming forth from the stillness, on its knowing itself in the kind of transhumanity – the "trasumanar" of *Paradiso* I.70 – as but humanity itself in act. Joy, in short, is but the mood of being in its proper exponentiality. It is but the *ecstatic* mood of being in its authenticity.

TWO

The *Vita Nova*

PRELIMINARY CONSIDERATIONS: NEW LIFE and a new
book – love and love-understanding: the pilgrim way – a
Commedia a minore.

PRELIMINARY CONSIDERATIONS: NEW LIFE AND A NEW BOOK

The *Vita nova* – the exquisite *Vita nova* – is the great book of Dante's early period as a poet and philosopher, 'great' not least in its presiding both critically and creatively over the romance-vernacular tradition of versemaking in which it stands: 'critically' in the sense of weighing up the equality of each successive moment of that tradition to the – as Dante himself puts it in the *Purgatorio* – "dittar dentro" or innermost rhythm of love-discerning and love-understanding in the mind of the lover, and 'creatively' in the sense of fashioning a new kind of literary utterance, a discourse circling securely about the still centre of its own concern.

Taking first, then, the critical as distinct from the creative moment of the argument we may say this: that at the head of the tradition within which he himself was at work stand those poets more or less closely associated with the court of the Hohenstaufen emperor Frederick II in Palermo, poets in turn busy within a tradition of Occitanic or Provençal versemaking. So, for example, as far as the Sicilians are concerned, a Giacomo da Lentini or a Guido delle Colonne or a Rinaldo d'Aquino, each alike an able administrator of the *topoi* of Provençal lyricism but for all that nicely focused with respect to the substance and psychology of love as a disposition of the spirit. And what applies to the Sicilians at work in the early part of the thirteenth century applies also to their Tuscan successors at work in its middle years, where in response, however, to the exigencies of a more properly communal as distinct from courtly consciousness the psychological tends to shade off into the moral as a dominant preoccupation, and the perfect poise of the Sicilian line into something approaching a species of mannerism. With what amounts, then, albeit with the occasional exception, to a triumph of style over substance, we come to the next phase of the Italian lyric tradition, to – again as Dante himself puts it in the *Purgatorio* – the "dolce stil novo" or "sweet new style" registering as the terminology suggests a systematic renewal of the poetic enterprise at the levels both of understanding and of expression. To the fore, then, among the advocates of the new way, and indeed its principal architect and chief spokesman, was the in every sense larger than life figure of Guido Cavalcanti, larger than life both socially and, in respect of his subsisting somewhere on the far limits of contemporary Aristotelianism, spiritually. No less developed, however, was his instinct for the purity of the line, for the sound and syntax of the poetic period as transparent to the innermost movement of thought, and it was this that, by way of a complex process of action and reaction – of 'action' in respect of form in the newfound integrity thereof and of 'reaction' in respect of Cavalcanti's nonetheless insistent sense of love as but a principle of moral and intellectual distraction, indeed of moral and intellectual destruction – that encouraged Dante in a fresh exploration of love in its essential nature and finality and of the ways and means of its orderly articulation.

First, then, as far as Dante himself is concerned – and proceeding here by way of an ideal chronology of these things – comes his correspondence with Dante da Maiano, the barely disguised levity of his namesake when it comes to love and love making enjoying in Alighieri a nothing if not high-minded response, a preliminary statement of love as, whatever else it is, a matter of moral and intellectual virtue. Then, in what amounts to a further interrogation of his peers and predecessors with respect to the substance and psychology of love precisely as such, come (*a*) the suffering-and-perplexity-in-love poems conceived and composed first under the aegis of Guittone d'Arezzo as the leading light of Tuscan lyricism (where it is a question of rehearsing the at once plaintive and petitionary substance of unrequited love), and then of Cavalcanti (where it is a question of love's impossible paradoxes, of its power both to excite and to extinguish the spirit); and (*b*) those poems reflecting the altogether gentler disposition of the Bolognese poet Guido Guinizzelli (where albeit in a preliminary fashion it is a question of love less of possession than of praise, and thus, by way of praise, of a more radiant humanity) – all this, therefore, containing within itself an invitation to fresh scrutiny, to an ironing out of love's endless contradictions in favour of a more properly developed sense of its power to new life. This, then, is the task of the *Vita nova* as accommodating along the way every kind of moral, intellectual and emotional difficulty while at the same time distilling from it all a now coherent understanding of love as a principle of emergence, as that whereby the lover knows himself as but a new creation.

But that, where the *Vita nova* is concerned, is not all, for coming now to the creative as distinct from the critical aspect of the argument, what we have here over and beyond a nothing if not stringent interrogation of the tradition in which it stands is a new kind of literary utterance; for while in the course of the text Dante avails himself of just about the entire apparatus of high-scholastic disquisition – of the glossatorial and scholiastic techniques of the philosophical and theological luminaries of the time, not to mention the *divisiones textus* and technical procedures of the poets and rhetoricians – what we have here is by no means a mere *commentum* after the manner of, say, a Thomas Aquinas or an Albert the Great, nor even a mere *prosimetrum* after the manner of Boethius (each alike prominent among the most cherished of Dante's *auctores*), but something closer to what he himself calls a 'little book', a '*libello*'. What we have here in other words, in a text turning steadily about its own still centre of concern, its now secure sense of love properly understood as a principle of self-transcendence on the part of the lover, is a fresh species of writing and writerliness, a properly speaking *authorial* initiative in all the courage and consistency thereof.

LOVE AND LOVE-UNDERSTANDING: THE PILGRIM WAY

First, then, turning now to the course of the argument, comes the childhood encounter, an encounter, however, explored as far as Beatrice is concerned by way pre-eminently of the iconic and symbolic, and, as far as Dante is concerned, by way of the psychological trauma of it all, of love's dramatic inception. On the one hand, then, Beatrice, as yet in her ninth year, nobly attired in a delicate yet decorous crimson, and, above all, apparitional, a special presence:

> Nove fiate già appresso lo mio nascimento era tornato lo cielo de la luce quasi a uno medesimo punto, quanto a la sua propria girazione, quando a li miei occhi apparve prima la gloriosa donna de la mia mente, la quale fu chiamata da molti Beatrice, li quali non sapeano che si chiamare. Ella era in questa vita già stata tanto, che ne lo suo tempo lo cielo stellato era mosso verso la parte d'oriente de le dodici parti l'una d'un grado, sì che quasi dal principio del suo anno nono apparve a me, ed io la vidi quasi da la fine del mio nono. Apparve vestita di nobilissimo colore, umile e onesto, sanguigno, cinta e ornata a la guisa che a la sua giovanissima etade si convenia.

> Nine times since my birth the heaven of light had come back to just about the same point when the glorious lady of my mind – she whom many, little knowing what it meant to speak thus, called Beatrice – first appeared before my eyes. She had been in this life for just so long as it took the starry heaven to move eastwards by the twelfth part of one degree, so that she appeared to me just about at the beginning of her ninth year, I for my part seeing her towards the end of my own ninth

year. She appeared dressed in noblest colour, a modest and discreet crimson, girded and adorned in a manner becoming her tender age.

(*Vita nova* ii.1–3)

while on the other, Dante himself, who, under the sway now of Amore as from this point onwards the master of his soul, knows himself only in the perturbation of his vital spirits, of the *life-spirit* dwelling in the heart and quickening by way of the arteries the various functions of the body, of the *animal spirit* dwelling in the brain and served by the various organs of sense perception, and of the *natural spirit* dwelling in the liver and responsible for nourishing the whole in its proper operation – his in this sense being but an intimation of bane and blessing in, strange to say, their mutual in-abiding:

In quello punto dico veracemente che lo spirito de la vita, lo quale dimora ne la secretissima camera de lo cuore, cominciò a tremare sì fortemente che appariâ ne li menimi polsi orribilmente; e tremando disse queste parole: "Ecce deus fortior me, qui veniens dominabitur mihi". In quello punto lo spirito animale, lo quale dimora ne l'alta camera ne la quale tutti li spiriti sensitivi portano le loro percezioni, si cominciò a maravigliare molto, e parlando spezialmente a li spiriti del viso, sì disse queste parole: "Apparuit iam beatitudo vestra". In quello punto lo spirito naturale, lo quale dimora in quella parte ove si ministra lo nutrimento nostro, cominciò a piangere, e piangendo, disse queste parole: "Heu miser, quia frequenter impeditus ero deinceps!"

At that moment I say in all truth that the vital spirit which lives in the innermost chamber of the heart began to tremble so violently that I felt that trembling fearfully in the least of my pulses, uttering as it did so these words: "Behold a god more powerful than I, who, coming upon me, will rule over me." At that moment the animal spirit which lives in the uppermost chamber to which every sensitive spirit conveys its perception, began to wonder deeply, and, addressing in particular the spirit of sight, said these words: "Behold now your blessedness displayed"; whereupon the natural spirit which lives in the part where we are nourished, began to weep, and, weeping, spoke thus: "Woe is me, for mine, henceforth, will be but impediment!"

(*Vita nova* ii.4–6)

What, then, amounts in these preliminary chapters of the text to an account of the fraught psychology of the encounter – 'fraught' in the degree to which an intimation of bliss is informed in the self-same moment by fear and trembling – continues into the next, where just for an instant, however, anguish gives way to ecstasy as a dominant state of mind; for all in good time, Beatrice, of her goodness, bestows upon him her greeting, whereupon his joy, Dante says, knows no bounds:

Poi che furono passati tanti die, che appunto erano compiuti li nove anni appresso l'apparimento soprascritto di questa gentilissima, ne l'ultimo di questi die avvenne che questa mirabile donna apparve a me vestita di colore bianchissimo, in mezzo a due gentili donne, le quali erano di più lunga etade; e passando per una via, volse li occhi verso quella parte ov'io era molto pauroso, e per la sua ineffabile cortesia, la quale è oggi meritata nel grande secolo, mi salutoe molto virtuosamente, tanto che me parve allora vedere tutti li termini de la beatitudine.

With the passing of time, of nine years, in fact, since the aforesaid appearance of this, the most noble of women, it happened that this most wondrous lady appeared to me once more, clothed in pure white and walking between two no less noble ladies but of greater age; and as she passed by she turned her eyes to where in fear and trembling I myself was standing, whereupon, from out of her unspeakable goodness – a goodness

now rewarded in heaven – she greeted me so graciously that,
or so it seemed, my bliss knew no bounds.

(*Vita nova* iii.1)

Inebriated, then, in the sense of drunken in the spirit (the "come
inebriato mi partio da le genti" of iii.2), he retreats in keeping with
the gospel admonition into the privacy of his own space, there
to ponder afresh the rare substance of the encounter (the "ricorsi
a lo solingo luogo d'una camera, e puosimi a pensare di questa
cortesissima" of the same chapter), all, however, in what comes next,
not going according to plan; for catching wind of his preoccupation
with not one, in fact, but two "screen ladies" or "donne schermo"
(a strategy, Dante says, designed to divert attention from the true
object of his love), Beatrice denies him her greeting, constraining
him as she does so to a fundamental rethinking of the whole issue,
to a fresh account of love's essential nature and finality. First, then,
comes the tortured psychology of it all, the pain and perplexity
always and everywhere engendered by love's endless paradoxes, by
its promising one thing and delivering another:

Appresso di questa soprascritta visione, avendo già dette le
parole che Amore m'avea imposte a dire, mi cominciaro molti
e diversi pensamenti a combattere ed a tentare, ciascuno quasi
indefensibilemente; tra li quali pensamenti quattro mi parea
che ingombrassero più lo riposo de la vita. L'uno de li quali
era questo: buona è la signoria d'Amore, però che trae lo
intendimento del suo fedele da tutte le vili cose. L'altro era
questo: non buona è la signoria d'Amore, però che quanto lo
suo fedele più fede li porta, tanto più gravi e dolorosi punti
li conviene passare. L'altro era questo: lo nome d'Amore è
sì dolce a udire, che impossibile mi pare che la sua propria
operazione sia ne le più cose altro che dolce, con ciò sia cosa
che li nomi seguitino le nominate cose, sì come è scritto:
"Nomina sunt consequentia rerum". Lo quarto era questo:
la donna per cui Amore ti stringe così, non è come l'altre

donne, che leggeramente si muova dal suo cuore. E ciascuno mi combattea tanto, che mi facea stare quasi come colui che non sa per qual via pigli lo suo cammino, e che vuole andare e non sa onde se ne vada; e se io pensava di volere cercare una comune via di costoro, cioè là ove tutti s'accordassero, questa era via molto inimica verso me, cioè di chiamare e di mettermi ne le braccia de la Pietà.

It was after this vision that, having written after the manner Love had commanded, varied thoughts began to contend and strive one with another within me, each of them just about unanswerable. Four in particular of them seemed most to disturb my peace of mind. One of them was this: Love's lordship is a good thing because he deters the mind of those who follow him faithfully from all unworthiness. Another was this: Love's governance is not good because the more faithful his follower, the greater the pain and the misery he must endure. The third was as follows: the name Love is so sweet to hear that – or so it seems to me – it is impossible that its general effect can be anything other than sweet, since in keeping with the formula "Names follow upon things themselves" it is well known that the name of a thing derives from what that thing is. The fourth was this: the lady through whom Love constrains you so is not like other ladies whose hearts are easily swayed. Each of these thoughts so contended within me, that I was like one uncertain of which road to take, like one anxious to set out but not knowing where to start. And if I cast about to see how they might after all be reconciled, some way, that is to say, in which they all might be made to agree, the only way I could see – abhorrent to me as it was – was to call upon Pity and throw myself into her arms.

(*Vita nova* xiii.1–6)

– lines to which, as marking the *non plus ultra* of Dante's anguish, we may add these from Chapter xiv, the chapter of the *gabbo* or jest, lines registering the humiliation of being mocked, not simply by his lady, but by the substance of his own love-understanding, a situation from which – short of a fundamental restructuring of self on the planes of seeing, knowing and desiring – there can be no hope of return:

> Io dico che molte di queste donne, accorgendosi de la mia trasfigurazione, si cominciaro a maravigliare, e ragionando si gabbavano di me con questa gentilissima; onde lo ingannato amico di buona fede mi prese per la mano, e traendomi fuori de la veduta di queste donne, sì mi domandò che io avesse. Allora io, riposato alquanto, e resurressiti li morti spiriti miei ... dissi a questo mio amico queste parole: "Io tenni li piedi in quella parte de la vita di là da la quale non si puote ire più per intendimento di ritornare".

> A good number of those women present, seeing the change that had come over me, were overcome with astonishment, and, discussing it among themselves, they, together with this most gracious lady, began mocking me; whereupon my friend, who though in good faith had been unwise enough to bring me along, took me by the hand and led me from the sight of those women, enquiring of me what was wrong, I for my part, having recovered myself a little and revived my lifeless spirits, ... said to my friend: "I have set foot in that part of life beyond which there is no going with any hope of returning."

> (*Vita nova* xiv.7–8)

But then, in the wake of despair thus understood, comes just such a moment of restructuring, a thinking through of the love-problematic apt to issue in a fresh sense of love as the in-and-through-which of a more spacious humanity, of a humanity, that is to say, more properly equal to the to-and-fro rhythm of pain and pleasure. True, the sign-posting hereabouts, if by 'sign-posting' we mean Dante's sudden announcement in Chapter xvii to the effect that, having now spoken enough of himself, he has it in mind to speak of something altogether more noble, is peremptory in the extreme; but this is peremptoriness with a purpose, peremptoriness designed straightaway to mark the difference, to signal the eclipse of the old by the new:

Poi che dissi questi tre sonetti, ne li quali parlai a questa donna però che fuoro narratori di tutto quasi lo mio stato, credendomi tacere e non dire più però che mi parea di me assai avere manifestato, avvegna che sempre poi tacesse di dire a lei, a me convenne ripigliare matera nuova e più nobile che la passata. E però che la cagione de la nuova matera è dilettevole a udire, la dicerò, quanto potrò più brievemente.

With the composition of these three sonnets – sonnets addressed to this lady and informing her of my condition in just about its entirety – I thought it right then to hold my peace and say no more, for it seemed to me that, even though this meant no longer addressing her further, I had spoken sufficiently of myself, and that it was time now to broach a new and nobler theme than hitherto. And since the occasion of my lighting on this new theme is agreeable to the ear, I shall speak of it as briefly as I am able.

What comes next, then, by way of the point-about-which of Dante's entire meditation in the *Vita nova* is a sort of *sacra rappresentazione*, sacred in the degree to which, by way of an again nicely judged combination of seeing and saying, of philosophical *nous* and narrative economy, Dante communicates a now revised sense of what it means to love and to love well, namely to rejoice in the other and greater than self as the way of finding self, of, in short, knowing self in the now and henceforth ecstatic substance thereof:

Le donne erano molte, tra le quali n'avea certe che si rideano tra loro; altre v'erano che mi guardavano aspettando che io dovessi dire; altre v'erano che parlavano tra loro. De le quali una, volgendo li suoi occhi verso me e chiamandomi per nome, disse queste parole: "A che fine ami tu questa tua donna, poi

che tu non puoi sostenere la sua presenza? Dilloci, ché certo
lo fine di cotale amore conviene che sia novissimo". E poi che
m'ebbe dette queste parole, non solamente ella, ma tutte l'altre
cominciaro ad attendere in vista la mia risponsione. Allora dissi
queste parole loro: "Madonne, lo fine del mio amore fue già lo
saluto di questa donna, forse di cui voi intendete, e in quello
dimorava la beatitudine, ché era fine di tutti li miei desiderii.
Ma poi che le piacque di negarlo a me, lo mio segnore Amore,
la sua merzede, ha posto tutta la mia beatitudine in quello che
non mi puote venire meno". Allora queste donne cominciaro
a parlare tra loro; e sì come talora vedemo cadere l'acqua
mischiata di bella neve, così mi parea udire le loro parole uscire
mischiate di sospiri. E poi che alquanto ebbero parlato tra loro,
anche mi disse questa donna che m'avea prima parlato, queste
parole: "Noi ti preghiamo che tu ne dichi ove sta questa tua
beatitudine". Ed io, rispondendo lei, dissi cotanto: "In quelle
parole che lodano la donna mia".

The ladies were many, some laughing among themselves,
others looking at me waiting to hear what I would say, and
others again talking among themselves. Of these, one, turning
her eyes towards me and calling me by name, spoke thus:
"What, since you are unable to endure her presence, can be the
object of your love for this, your lady? Do tell us, since the aim
of such love must indeed be very strange", whereupon, having
spoken these words, not only she but all the others seemed
from their expression to await my reply. I, then, addressed
her thus: "My lady, the aim of my love was once that lady's
greeting – the lady whereof you perhaps know – and in that
greeting dwelt my every blessedness, the object in turn of my
every desiring. But since she saw fit to deny me her greeting,
my lord Love, in his mercy, has placed all my happiness in that
which cannot fail me." At this, those ladies began to speak
among themselves: and as we sometimes see beautiful flakes
of snow mixed in with the rain as it falls, so I seemed to hear
their words mingled with sighs. And when they had spoken a

while among themselves, the lady who had addressed me first spoke to me saying: "Tell us, we beg you, wherein lies your blessedness." And I, in reply, said: "In those words praising my lady."

(*Vita nova* xviii.3–6)

Consummate as it is in its intermingling of the dramatic and the dialectical, of the idea pure and simple and of the *mise en scène* as the means of its contemplation, the passage testifies also to the most complete kind of cultural appropriation, to an interweaving of any number of hallowed emphases for the purposes of producing a now seamless garment. Everything is there, from the Psalmist on the new song (Ps. 33:1–3; 40:3) to Luke (10:42) on the better part that cannot be taken away and Paul (Romans 12:2 and 2 Cor. 5:17) on the new creation; from Aristotle (*Ethics* viii.3; 1156b6–11) to Cicero (*De amicitia* ix.31) on friendship as a matter of disinterested concern; from Bernard (*De diligendo Deo* vii) to Aelred (*De spirituali amicitia* i) on the love that seeks not its own; and from Boethius (*Consolatio philosophiae* II. pr. iv) to – nicely – Jean de Meun on love as a condition of the spirit indifferent to fortune and the whole thing, therefore, as but a matter of stable self-possession:

> touz les biens que dedanz toi senz
> et que si bien les connois enz,
> qui te demeurent sanza cessier
> si qu'il ne te peuent lessier
> por fere a autre autel servise:
> cist bient sunt tien a droite guise.

Whatever of worth you have within you and that you recognize as truly your own, and that remains always with you, never taking leave of you to enter another's service, that is rightly and properly yours.

(*Roman de la rose*, 5301–5306)

But the resourcefulness of the text, its weaving from any number of golden threads an again seamless garment of love-understanding, is as nothing when compared with the garment itself, with, in this eighteenth chapter of the *libello*, a narrative as sublime in conception as it is gracious in expression. And it is Dante's sense of love as a principle of self-transcendence in point both of knowing and of desiring, as that whereby the lover knows himself in the revised shape and substance of self, that quickens and sustains the great praise poems of the *Vita nova* in all their now hymnic intensity; so, for example, these lines from the aesthetic moment of the great inaugural canzone, *Donne ch'avete intelletto d'amore*, from that part of the poem looking to celebrate Beatrice's goodness by way of her beauty:

> Dice di lei Amor: "Cosa mortale
> come esser pò sì adorna e sì pura?".
> Poi la reguarda, e fra se stesso giura
> che Dio ne 'ntenda di far cosa nova.
>   Color di perle ha quasi in forma, quale
> convene a donna aver, non for misura;
> ella è quanto de ben pò far natura;
> per esemplo di lei bieltà si prova.
>   De li occhi suoi, come ch'ella li mova,
> escono spirti d'amore inflammati,
> che feron li occhi a qual che allor la guati,
>   e passan sì che 'l cor ciascun retrova:
> voi le vedete Amor pinto nel viso,
> là 've non pote alcun mirarla fiso.

Of her Love says: "Whence this beauty and purity in a mortal being?" Then, looking upon her, he avows within him that God intends here a miracle. Pearl in complexion is she, but discreetly so as becomes a woman. She is the sum of everything of which nature is capable, and, exemplary as she is, the measure of all beauty whatever. Forth from her eyes wherever she bends her gaze come spirits flaming with the power of love, striking as they do so those eyes in turn gazing upon her and making their way within until they find the heart. Look and you will see love depicted upon her face, there where no man dare linger with his gaze.

(*Donne ch'avete intelletto d'amore*, lines 43–56)

while following on among the handmaidens of *Donne ch'avete* and constituting within the economy of the text as a whole the first fruits thereof is the sonnet *Tanto gentile e onesta pare*, a sonnet worth pausing over precisely for its status as but an essay in praise – in the opening out of self upon the other and upon the greater than self – in its now pure form:

> Tanto gentile e tanto onesta pare
> la donna mia, quand'ella altrui saluta,
> ch'ogne lingua deven tremando muta,
> e li occhi no l'ardiscon di guardare.
>   Ella si va, sentendosi laudare,
> benignamente d'umiltà vestuta;
> e par che sia una cosa venuta
> da cielo in terra a miracol mostrare.
>   Mòstrasi sì piacente a chi la mira,
> che dà per li occhi una dolcezza al core,
> che 'ntender no la può chi non la prova:
>   e par che de la sua labbia si mova
> un spirito soave pien d'amore,
> che va dicendo a l'anima: "Sospira!"

So noble and so full of dignity my lady appears when she greets anyone that all tongues tremble and fall silent, and eyes dare not look upon her. She goes on her way, hearing herself praised, graciously clothed with humility, and seems a creature come down from heaven to earth to make known the miraculous. She appears so beautiful to those who gaze upon her that through the eyes she sends a sweetness into the heart such as none can understand but he who experiences it; and

from her lips seems to come a spirit, gentle and full of love,
that says to the soul: "Sigh!"

It is, then, at this point – at the point of self as summoned by
way of love as a matter of praise to the most radical kind of self-
surpassing or self-surmounting (the "sormontar" of *Paradiso* XXX)
in point of knowing and loving – that the hymnic shades off into
the Christic, into a sense, not certainly of the *identity* of Beatrice
and the Christ, but of their *analogy* or of the likeness that might be
said to subsist between them. The key text here, notable not least
for its now definitive location of the Cavalcantian *vis-à-vis* the
Dantean (Cavalcanti's Giovanna being to Dante's Beatrice as but
one making straight the way of the Lord), runs as follows:

> ... io vidi venire verso me una gentile donna, la quale era di
> famosa bieltade, e fue già molto donna di questo primo mio
> amico. E lo nome di questa donna era Giovanna, salvo che
> per la sua bieltade, secondo che altri crede, imposto l'era nome
> Primavera; e così era chiamata. E appresso lei, guardando, vidi
> venire la mirabile Beatrice. Queste donne andaro presso di
> me così l'una appresso l'altra, e parve che Amore mi parlasse
> nel cuore, e dicesse: "Quella prima è nominata Primavera
> solo per questa venuta d'oggi; ché io mossi lo imponitore del
> nome a chiamarla così Primavera, cioè prima verrà lo die che
> Beatrice si mosterrà dopo la imaginazione del suo fedele. E
> se anche vogli considerare lo primo nome suo, tanto è quanto
> dire 'prima verrà', però che lo suo nome Giovanna è da quello
> Giovanni lo quale precedette la verace luce, dicendo: 'Ego vox
> clamantis in deserto: parate viam Domini'".

> ... I saw coming towards me a noble lady, one famous for her
> beauty and who had long since been beloved of my closest
> friend. Her name was Giovanna, but because of her beauty
> she had as some say been given the name Primavera, and was
> known as such. And as I watched I saw coming after her the
> miraculous Beatrice. These ladies passed close by me one after

the other, at which point Love seemed to say in my heart: "The lady you see first is called Primavera, the name which I, with this very procession in mind, inspired in the one who first called her thus; for she it is who, on the day of Beatrice's self-revelation hard upon the vision of her faithful servant, will precede her. And if, moreover, you give heed to her real name, Giovanna, that also means 'she who comes first', since Giovanna comes from Giovanni, from the one who preceded the true light saying: 'I am the voice of one crying in the wilderness: prepare the way of the Lord.'"

(*Vita nova* xxiv. 3–4)

Now here, clearly, we have once again to be careful, for taking the *Vita nova* in the round, there can be no question of fashioning from it a work of specifically Christian piety; for within the economy of the whole the Christic, called upon as it is to help resolve a set of literary and literary-aesthetic issues in the area of romance-vernacular versemaking, serves the purposes less of the Christian than of the courtly as but a precise set of cultural concerns. But for all that, the analogy is there and there insistently, for as Dante himself is at pains to make clear it is a question where Beatrice is concerned, not merely of her Christ-like *presence* (the "da cielo in terra a miracol mostrare" of *Tanto gentile e tanto onesta pare*), but of her Christ-like *operation* (the "ella mirabilemente operando" of xxi. 1), these between them, for all their falling short of identity as distinct from mere resemblance, witnessing nonetheless to an order of experimentation at the very far limits of notional and expressive possibility.

Experimentation at the limits of notional and expressive possibility notwithstanding, however, the *Vita nova* as a study in the better part that cannot be taken away awaits its final denouement, death and the anguish thereof now moving centre-stage as a necessary condition of that denouement. And here again Dante's handling of yet another complex phase of the argument is consummate, any suggestion of death as but interruption on the plane, so to speak, of the horizontal being straightaway taken up in a wholly more considered sense of its status as a component of love-intelligence, as that whereby love properly understood might be said to transcend its mere occasions, the to-and-fro agony and ecstasy of its positive living out. In the midst, therefore, of his rejoicing – strategically located, that is to say, between *Donne ch'avete intelletto d'amore* on the one hand and *Tanto gentile e tanto onesta pare* on the other – intimations of death intervene to deepen and differentiate the argument, to encourage a still more seasoned reflection upon the substance and significance of love as a principle of self-interpretation. First, then, comes the death of Beatrice's father in Chapter xxii, nicely attentive, to be sure, in registering the funerary customs of contemporary Florence but serving for the moment to insinuate a fresh set of considerations, to refine still further the substance of love-understanding:

E con ciò sia cosa che, secondo l'usanza de la sopradetta cittade, donne con donne e uomini con uomini s'adunino a cotale tristizia, molte donne s'adunaro colà dove questa Beatrice piangea pietosamente; onde io veggendo ritornare alquante donne da lei, udio dicere loro parole di questa gentilissima, com'ella si lamentava; tra le quali parole udio che diceano: "Certo ella piange sì, che quale la mirasse doverebbe morire di pietade". Allora trapassaro queste donne; e io rimasi in tanta tristizia, che alcuna lagrima talora bagnava la mia faccia, onde io mi ricopria con porre le mani spesso a li miei occhi; e se non fosse ch'io attendea audire anche di lei, però ch'io era in luogo onde se ne giano la maggior parte di quelle donne che da lei si partiano, io mi sarei nascoso incontanente che le lagrime m'aveano assalito.

Since it is the custom of the aforesaid city for women to foregather with women, and men with men, on such sad occasions, a good number of women met together there where Beatrice was most piteously weeping; whereupon I, seeing some of them making their way back, heard them talking among themselves of how she mourned, and of what they were saying I was able to make out the following: "Such indeed is her weeping that simply to see her would be to die of compassion." With this, they went their way, I for my part, however, being so overcome with sadness that tears flowed from my eyes, whence I repeatedly covered them with my hands. And were it not that I awaited further news of my lady (for most of the women, in taking their leave of her, would come my way) I would have hidden myself away for the grief that had overtaken me.

(*Vita nova* xxii.3–4)

But then, hard on the heels of the anticipatory comes the apocalyptic, the hallucinatory, the terrifying intuition of death – to wit, that of Beatrice herself – as now close to home, at which point love-awareness, hitherto a matter of madonna's positive presence to the lover, begins to open out upon sorrowing as but part and parcel of its deep substance:

Appresso ciò per pochi dì, avvenne che in alcuna parte de la mia persona mi giunse una dolorosa infermitade, onde io continuamente soffersi per nove dì amarissima pena; la quale mi condusse a tanta debolezza, che me convenia stare come coloro li quali non si possono muovere. Io dico che ne lo nono giorno, sentendome dolere quasi intollerabilemente, a me giunse uno pensero, lo quale era de la mia donna. E quando ei pensato alquanto di lei, ed io ritornai pensando a la mia debilitata vita; e veggendo come leggero era lo suo durare, ancora che sana fosse, sì cominciai a piangere fra me stesso di tanta miseria. Onde, sospirando forte, dicea fra me medesimo: "Di necessitade convene che la gentilissima Beatrice alcuna volta si muoia".

It happened a few days after this that I was in a certain part of my body sorely afflicted, my pain being such that for a good nine days I was drained of all energy and obliged to lie still like one unable to move. Then on the ninth day, suffering as I was intolerably, a thought came to me of my lady. And when I had reflected on her for a while, I fell to thinking again about my own enfeebled existence, and, pondering its ephemerality even in the best of circumstances, I began weeping at the wretchedness of it all; whence, sighing deeply, I said to myself: "One day, but of necessity, the noble Beatrice too will have to die."

(*Vita nova* xxiii.1–3)

It is at this point, then, that death – meaning by this the death of the beloved – mounts yet a further challenge to the lover's understanding of what in truth love actually is, of, more exactly, its status as a condition of the spirit equal to its every eventuality. And it is at this point, or, rather, at the point of Beatrice's actual demise a little way down the line, that Dante pauses to do two things decisive for any overall interpretation of the *Vita nova*; namely (*a*) to stress that it is indeed *understanding* rather than *eventuality* that actually matters here, and (*b*) to confirm the equality of the vernacular as equal to the matter in hand, to discourse at the point of ultimate concern. On the one hand, then, the event itself, solemn to be sure in its announcement but sidelined just about immediately in favour of what for the Dante of the *Vita nova* most matters about it, namely its consequences for a continuing process of love-intelligence:

Quomodo sedet sola civitas plena populo! facta est quasi vidua domina gentium. Io era nel proponimento ancora di questa canzone, e compiuta n'avea questa soprascritta stanzia, quando lo segnore de la giustizia chiamoe questa gentilissima a gloriare sotto la insegna di quella regina benedetta virgo Maria, lo cui nome fue in grandissima reverenzia ne le parole di questa Beatrice beata. E avvegna che forse piacerebbe a presente trattare alquanto de la sua partita da noi, non è lo mio intendimento di trattarne qui per tre ragioni: la prima è che ciò non è del presente proposito, se volemo guardare nel proemio che precede questo libello ... e però lascio cotale trattato ad altro chiosatore.

How doth the city sit solitary, that was full of people. How is she become a widow! I was busy composing this canzone and had just completed the above stanza, when the lord of all justice called this most gracious of women to glory under the insignia of that queen, the Blessed Virgin Mary, whose name was forever, and with the greatest reverence, upon the lips of the blessed Beatrice. And although it might perhaps be welcome were I at present to say something of her departure from us, it is not my intention here so to do, and this for three reasons: the first is that, for anyone caring to look back to the preface of this, my little book, to speak thus of Beatrice's departure is no part of my present purpose ... I therefore leave this for another to comment on.

(*Vita nova* xxviii.1–2)

while on the other hand, and as reaching down into the very recesses of Dante's sensibility and indeed of his very being as a poet, philosopher and ultimately prophet in the *lingua di sì*, the vernacular moment of the argument, its commitment here as in the as yet far-off *Convivio* and *Commedia* to the tongue properly his own as the form of ontic awareness, as that whereby the innermost substance of self is raised up and proposed as an object of contemplation. Ancillary concerns too – namely friendship and the intimations of one Guido Cavalcanti – have their part to play here, but they are indeed ancillary, the vernacular itself, in all its now perfect equality and indeed perfect proportionality to the matter in hand, determining the course of the argument:

Poi che fue partita da questo secolo, rimase tutta la sopradetta cittade quasi vedova dispogliata da ogni dignitade; onde io, ancora lagrimando in questa desolata cittade, scrissi a li prìncipi de la terra alquanto de la sua condizione, pigliando quello cominciamento di Geremia profeta che dice: *Quomodo sedet sola civitas.* E questo dico, acciò che altri non si maravigli perché io l'abbia allegato di sopra, quasi come entrata de la nuova materia che appresso vene. E se alcuno volesse me riprendere di ciò, ch'io non scrivo qui le parole che seguitano a quelle allegate, escusomene, però che lo intendimento mio non fue dal principio di scrivere altro che per volgare: onde, con ciò sia cosa che le parole che seguitano a quelle che sono allegate siano tutte latine, sarebbe fuori del mio intendimento se le scrivessi. E simile intenzione so ch'ebbe questo mio primo amico a cui io ciò scrivo, cioè ch'io li scrivessi solamente volgare.

After she had departed this life, the entire city of which I have spoken was left as though widowed, despoiled of all worth, so that I, grieving still in that desolate place, wrote to the rulers of the land intimating something of her condition, taking as my beginning the words of the prophet Jeremiah *How solitary doth the city sit.* And I say this so that no one might be surprised at my quoting them again as a sort of heading to the fresh material now following. And should anyone wish to reproach me with not writing out the words following on from this text, my reason for not doing so is that it was only ever my intention here to write in the vernacular, quoting the rest of the Latin text thus being contrary to my original plan. Neither is it lost on me that setting the entire work down in the vernacular was the wish too of my closest friend, of the one for whom I write this book.

(*Vita nova* xxx)

But that is not all, for the *purgatorialità* of the *Vita nova* – its sense, that is to say, of the sheer difficulty of it all, of love, properly understood, being but a mountain to climb – extends not only to bereavement but to temptation as a stumbling block, as apt to waylay even the most attentive lover. For bereft as he now is of Beatrice's presence, there is always the possibility of looking elsewhere, of seeking comfort by way of the sweet glances of another – the case, precisely, of Dante and the 'donna gentile' or compassionate lady of the casement. But here as always in the *Vita nova* we must tread carefully, for it is a question now not merely of alternativism pure and simple, of, in the context of bereavement, his merely looking for comfort elsewhere, but rather, and altogether more subtly, of his seeing in the compassionate lady of the casement a way back to Beatrice herself, of recovering as far as may be her material presence to him, the episode of the "donna gentile" thus constituting within the economy of the whole a final and nothing if not strenuous attempt to liquidate the notion of *seeing* as a condition of *loving* and thus of *being* in its at last paradisal perfection. First, then, the encounter itself, exquisite in its sense of compassion in the one who looks on as apt merely to intensify the rhythm of suffering in the already suffering spirit:

Poi per alquanto tempo, con ciò fosse cosa che io fosse in parte ne la quale mi ricordava del passato tempo, molto stava pensoso, e con dolorosi pensamenti, tanto che mi faceano parere de fore una vista di terribile sbigottimento. Onde io, accorgendomi del mio travagliare, levai li occhi per vedere se altri mi vedesse. Allora vidi una gentile donna giovane e bella molto, la quale da una finestra mi riguardava sì pietosamente, quanto a la vista, che tutta la pietà parea in lei accolta. Onde, con ciò sia cosa che quando li miseri veggiono di loro compassione altrui, più tosto si muovono a lagrimare, quasi come di se stessi avendo pietade, io senti' allora cominciare li miei occhi a volere piangere; e però, temendo di non mostrare la mia vile vita, mi partio dinanzi da li occhi di questa gentile …

Since but a little later I happened to be in a place calling to mind past times, I stood there lost in thought, my outward aspect, in consequence of my now grievous state of mind, being one of deep distress. Thus conscious of my suffering, I looked up to see if anyone else was likewise aware of it, whereupon I saw a noble and very lovely young woman looking so compassionately upon me that she seemed to be compassion incarnate. And just as, sensing the sympathy of those round about them, the wretched (almost as though having compassion upon themselves) are all the more ready to weep, so I felt my eyes brimming with tears; and so, fearing lest I reveal anything more of my own wretchedness, I departed from her sight ...

(*Vita nova* xxxv. 1–3)

but then, and no less exquisitely, the function of the encounter as, if only in a manner alert to the unreality and indeed to the impropriety of it all, a way back, a means of looking again upon the radiant complexion of Beatrice as that whereby the lover might sorrow all the more freely:

Avvenne poi che là ovunque questa donna mi vedea, sì si facea d'una vista pietosa e d'un colore palido quasi come d'amore; onde molte fiate mi ricordava de la mia nobilissima donna, che di simile colore si mostrava tuttavia. E certo molte volte non potendo lagrimare né disfogare la mia tristizia, io andava per vedere questa pietosa donna, la quale parea che tirasse le lagrime fuori de li miei occhi per la sua vista.

From then on wherever this lady saw me her expression grew compassionate and her face turned pale almost as though with love, reminding me most often of my noble lady who was always of a similar complexion. And often indeed, when I could not weep or give expression to my sorrow, I used to go and see this lady, the very sight of whom seemed to draw tears from my eyes.

(*Vita nova* xxxvi. 1–2)

But it is the unreality and indeed the impropriety of it all that, in circumstances of unspeakable psychological complexity, win through, what follows taking the form of a vitriolic indictment of the eyes as but a principle of forgetfulness, as, in respect of every more stable acquisition of the spirit, a mere distraction:

Io venni a tanto per la vista di questa donna, che li miei occhi si cominciaro a dilettare troppo di vederla; onde molte volte me ne crucciava nel mio cuore, ed aveamene per vile assai. Onde più volte bestemmiava la vanitade de li occhi miei, e dicea loro nel mio pensero: "Or voi solavate fare piangere chi vedea la vostra dolorosa condizione, ed ora pare che vogliate dimenticarlo per questa donna che vi mira; che non mira voi, se non in quanto le pesa de la gloriosa donna di cui piangere solete; ma quanto potete fate, ché io la vi pur rimembrerò molto spesso, maladetti occhi, ché mai, se non dopo la morte, non dovrebbero le vostre lagrime avere restate".

The sight of this lady began to have such an effect on me that my eyes began to delight too much in seeing her, whence, frequently taking myself to task within me, I held myself on this account to be the basest of men. Time and again I cursed the fickleness of my eyes, addressing them thus in conscience: "It was not long since you made those looking upon you weep for your sorrowful state, but now it seems that all you want is to put it out of your mind for this woman who gazes upon you, but this only insofar as she grieves for the now glorious lady for whom you yourself once wept. But have your own way, accursed eyes of mine, for I forever will remind you of her, your tears knowing of necessity no respite this side of death."

(*Vita nova* xxxvii. 1–2)

This, then, is what it means to speak of the episode of the "donna gentile" as both the final challenge to, and the final confirmation of, Dante's leading idea in the *Vita nova*, to wit the notion of love as engendered, to be sure, by the customary processes of perception, abstraction and intentionalization, but, once espoused as a principle of self-interpretation, as that whereby the individual knows self in the actuality of self, immune to the vagaries of sight and sound.

With what amounts, then, to a fresh and more than ever secure sense of the inwardness of it all, of love properly understood as a principle of ulterior being and becoming on the part of the lover, the *Vita nova* has run its course, Dante's only remaining task now being (*a*) to place on record the miraculous vision whereby he was confirmed afresh in a sense of her – Beatrice's – glory and of his unreason, (*b*) to endorse by way of the *romei* or of those making their way to Rome by way of Florence as a city in mourning the notion of love and love-understanding as a matter of spiritual journeying, and (*c*) to commit himself to a yet more adequate account of Beatrice and of the Beatrician as and when he feels himself to be more properly equal to the task. With respect, therefore, to the first of these things, the following lines from the beginning of Chapter xxxix, again nothing less than purgatorial in the depth and intensity of their self-interrogation:

Contra questo avversario de la ragione si levoe un die, quasi ne l'ora de la nona, una forte imaginazione in me; che mi parve vedere questa gloriosa Beatrice con quelle vestimenta sanguigne co le quali apparve prima a li occhi miei; e pareami giovane in simile etade in quale io prima la vidi. Allora cominciai a pensare di lei; e ricordandomi di lei secondo l'ordine del tempo passato, lo mio cuore cominciò dolorosamente a pentere de lo desiderio a cui sì vilmente s'avea lasciato possedere alquanti die contra la costanzia de la ragione; e discacciato questo cotale malvagio desiderio, sì si rivolsero tutti li miei pensamenti a la loro gentilissima Beatrice. E dico che d'allora innanzi cominciai a pensare di lei sì con tutto lo vergognoso cuore, che li sospiri manifestavano ciò molte volte; però che tutti quasi diceano nel loro uscire quello che nel cuore si ragionava, cioè lo nome di quella gentilissima, e come si partìo da noi.

Over and against this adversary of reason, there arose within me one day, at about the ninth hour, a mighty vision in which, clothed in the crimson dress in which she had first appeared to me and seeming as young as when we first met, I beheld

Beatrice in glory; whence I began thinking of her, and, recalling
her thus in the order of time passing, I began in my heart, with
much sorrowing, to repent of the desire to which, over against
the steady insistence of reason, I had delivered it. But now,
with the expulsion of this wretched desire, my every thought
turned back upon this, my most gracious Beatrice. From that
moment on, I say, I began to think on her with such shame in
my heart that my every sigh spoke of it, just about every one
of them bearing witness in its coming forth to the innermost
reasoning of my heart, to wit, the name of that most noble of
women and the manner of her departure.

(*Vita nova* xxxix. 1–3)

while with respect to the second of them these from the next
chapter, exquisite in their confirming by way of the pilgrim motif
the deep substance of the text as but an essay in spiritual wayfaring,
in the sorrowing, to be sure, but at the same time in the sublimity
of the upward way:

Dopo questa tribulazione avvenne, in quello tempo che molta
gente va per vedere quella imagine benedetta la quale Iesu
Cristo lasciò a noi per esemplo de la sua bellissima figura, la
quale vede la mia donna gloriosamente, che alquanti peregrini
passavano per una via la quale è quasi mezzo de la cittade
ove nacque e vivette e morìo la gentilissima donna. Li quali
peregrini andavano, secondo che mi parve, molto pensosi; ond'io
pensando a loro, dissi fra me medesimo: "Questi peregrini
mi paiono di lontana parte, e non credo che anche udissero
parlare di questa donna, e non ne sanno neente; anzi li loro
penseri sono d'altre cose che di queste qui, ché forse pensano
de li loro amici lontani, li quali noi non conoscemo". Poi dicea
fra me medesimo: "Io so che s'elli fossero di propinquo paese,
in alcuna vista parrebbero turbati passando per lo mezzo de la
dolorosa cittade". Poi dicea fra me medesimo: "Se io li potesse
tenere alquanto, io li pur farei piangere anzi ch'elli uscissero

di questa cittade, però che io direi parole le quali farebbero piangere chiunque le intendesse".

It so happened that, in the wake of this sorrowing and at that time of the year when many make their way to see the blessed likeness that Christ Jesus left us as an instance of his beautiful countenance (the countenance upon which even now my lady gazes in glory), some of their pilgrim number were passing along the way running just about through the centre of the city wherein the noblest of women was born, lived and died. They made their way, or so it seemed to me, deep in thought, whereupon, thinking of them, I said to myself: "These, it seems, are pilgrims from a far-off place such that, as I believe, they cannot have heard of that lady. Knowing nothing of her, their thoughts must be of things other than those living here, thoughts, perhaps, of distant friends, friends of whom we here know nothing." Then again I said to myself: "I know that if they were indeed from somewhere nearby they too, as they made their way through the middle of this city in mourning, would likewise appear distressed", saying further to myself: "If then I could detain them but for a moment I would cause them likewise to weep before departing the city, for I would speak unto them words apt to cause any hearing them to weep."

(*Vita nova* xl.1–4)

and finally, as regards the third of them, Dante's commitment to speak no more of Beatrice until such time as he is able to do so with greater authority, in a manner apt to honour more completely both the substance and implications of her presence to him as himself but a pilgrim spirit. In fact, by the time of the *Vita nova* as post-dating Beatrice's death by perhaps three or four years, he had already been busy about redefining the leading preoccupations and allegiances of his existence, matters very definitely other than Beatrician in kind now laying claim to his moral and intellectual energy. But for all that, and for all its characterization in the

Convivio as but the "fervent and passionate" expression of his early manhood (*Convivio* I.i.16), we have here even so testimony to a moment of resolution, a moment open, it is true, to refinement in point both of conception and of expression, but for all that a moment transparent to its own innermost reasons – a moment, in short, of blessed self-possession:

> Appresso questo sonetto, apparve a me una mirabile visione, ne la quale io vidi cose che mi fecero proporre di non dire più di questa benedetta, infino a tanto che io potesse più degnamente trattare di lei. E di venire a ciò io studio quanto posso, sì com'ella sae veracemente. Sì che, se piacere sarà di colui a cui tutte le cose vivono, che la mia vita duri per alquanti anni, io spero di dicer di lei quello che mai non fue detto d'alcuna. E poi piaccia a colui che è sire de la cortesia, che la mia anima se ne possa gire a vedere la gloria de la sua donna, cioè di quella benedetta Beatrice, la quale gloriosamente mira ne la faccia di colui *qui est per omnia secula benedictus.*

> After writing this sonnet a miraculous vision appeared to me, the contents of which made me determined to speak no further of this blessed lady until such time as I could do so more worthily. And as she herself well knows I am studying as hard as I can so that, should it please him by whom all things have life and breath that I myself live on a while, I hope to speak of her in a way no woman has ever been spoken of before. Whereafter, may it please him who is gracious above all that my soul might journey on to behold the glory of its lady, that is of that blessed Beatrice, who looks gloriously on the face of the One *who is throughout all ages blessed.*

> (*Vita nova* xlii)

A COMMEDIA *A MINORE*

What, then, are we to say of the *Vita nova*? In short, that like everything else in Dante it is a work of astonishing courage and commitment, of courage in the sense of its addressing foursquare the issues both of substance and of style raised by the tradition of neo-courtly versemaking within which it stands, and of commitment in its espousal of those same issues as duly resolved and refined in the forum of conscience as the means of significant self-interpretation. And this – this espousal of those same issues as duly resolved and refined in the forum of conscience as the means of significant self-interpretation – is what now matters about it; for given in the way we have just indicated his subsequent sense of the *libello* as but the fervent and passionate expression of his early manhood, what we have here, for all its as yet youthful intuition, is a *Commedia* in the making, an account of human experience under the aspect of alienation, of emancipation and of emergence – of hell, purgatory and paradise.

First, then – and here we are thinking of the "diverse thoughts striving mightily within me" passage of Chapter xiii together with the 'gabbo' or mockery sequence of Chapter xiv – comes the infernal moment of the text, 'infernal' in its sense of the confused and darkling character of it all, of knowing self only in the impossibly conflicted character of self. True, it is hardly a question here in the *Vita nova* of the kind of hubris whereby the creature rises up against the creator in a spirit of moral and ontological defiance. But for all that, it is, in this early phase of the *libello*, a question of self-centrality, of love as seeking its own, and thus of the lover as knowing himself in the psychopathology of these things, by way, that is to say, of the fear, the confusion, the inexplicability and, as the boundary condition of these things, the despair generated by this situation; so, for example, in addition to the aforementioned 'diverse thoughts' and 'mockery' moments of Dante's discourse, these lines from Chapter xvi as but an essay in the nightmare sensation of near-nothingness on the plane of properly human being:

Appresso ciò che io dissi questo sonetto, mi mosse una volontade di dire anche parole, ne le quali io dicesse quattro cose ancora sopra lo mio stato, le quali non mi parea che fossero manifestate ancora per me. La prima de le quali si è che molte volte io mi dolea, quando a mia memoria movesse la fantasia ad imaginare quale Amore mi facea. La seconda si è che Amore spesse volte di subito m'assalia sì forte, che 'n me non rimanea altro di vita se non un pensero che parlava di questa donna. La terza si è che quando questa battaglia d'Amore mi pugnava così, io mi movea quasi discolorito tutto per vedere questa donna, credendo che mi difendesse la sua veduta da questa battaglia, dimenticando quello che per appropinquare a tanta gentilezza m'addivenia. La quarta si è come cotale veduta non solamente non mi difendea, ma finalmente disconfiggea la mia poca vita.

No sooner had I finished writing this sonnet than the wish came over me to write yet another in which I would say four more things about my condition, things that it seemed to me I had not yet made clear. The first of these was that, whenever I called to mind and thought over afresh Love's treatment of me, I was sore distressed. The second was that Love so often and so savagely set about me that – other than those thoughts speaking of my lady – nothing within me was left alive. The third was that when Love thus assailed me, I, believing that to catch sight of her would ward off this attack, felt constrained even so – pallid as I was and oblivious to what always happened whenever I approached her in all her graciousness – to seek her out. The fourth is how that same glimpse of her not only failed to defend me but did away with what little life remained to me.

(*Vita nova* xvi. 1–5)

Here, however, as in the *Commedia* as but a still more sublime essay in spiritual journeying, homecoming is by way of the purgatoriality of it all, of the moment represented in the *Vita nova* by the life-and-death struggle of its protagonist positively to embrace and to live out a now revised understanding of love, a sense, that is to say, of love as a matter less of having than of being, less of possession than of praise and of all this entails by way of the soul's proper 'transhumanity' or self-surpassing in point of knowing and loving. On the one hand, then, there is the 'intimation of death' sequence of Chapter xxiii, intimations of death in all the apocalyptic terror thereof constraining the poet to yet a fresh thinking through of the whole issue, indeed to a reconstruction of his entire existence as a lover:

Io dico che ne lo nono giorno, sentendo me dolere quasi intollerabilmente, a me giunse uno pensero, lo quale era de la mia donna. E quando èi pensato alquanto di lei, ed io ritornai pensando a la mia debilitata vita; e veggendo come leggero era lo suo durare, ancora che sana fosse, sì cominciai a piangere fra me stesso di tanta miseria. Onde, sospirando forte, dicea fra me medesimo: "Di necessitade convene che la gentilissima Beatrice alcuna volta si muoia". E però mi giunse uno sì forte smarrimento, che chiusi li occhi e cominciai a travagliare sì come farnetica persona ed a imaginare in questo modo; che ne lo incominciamento de lo errare che fece la mia fantasia, apparvero a me certi visi di donne scapigliate, che mi diceano: "Tu pur morrai"; e poi, dopo queste donne, m'apparvero certi visi diversi e orribili a vedere, li quali mi diceano: "Tu se' morto". Così cominciando ad errare la mia fantasia, venni a quello ch'io non sapea ove io mi fosse; e vedere mi parea donne andare scapigliate piangendo per via, maravigliosamente triste; e pareami vedere lo sole oscurare, sì che le stelle si mostravano di colore ch'elle mi faceano giudicare che piangessero; e pareami che li uccelli volando per l'aria cadessero morti, e che fossero grandissimi terremuoti.

Then on the ninth day, while undergoing unendurable pain, a thought came to me of my lady. And when I had reflected on her a little, my thoughts turned to my own frail life, and, realizing its small chances of lasting, even with good health, I wept at the misery of it all. Sighing deeply, I said within myself: one day the noble Beatrice will be forced to die. At this I was overcome by such delirium that I shut my eyes and started to thrash about like one fevered. My imagination at the beginning of its wanderings thrust before me the faces of ladies with their hair dishevelled. They said to me: "You too shall die." Then after these ladies came more strange and terrifying faces, which said: "You are dead." Owing to the vagaries of my imagination, I did not know where I was, and I thought I saw ladies wandering along a road, their hair tumbling down and sad beyond belief. Then I saw the sun darkened and the stars changed to such a colour that I thought they wept; birds dropped dead while flying through the air, and there were vast earthquakes.

(Vita nova xxiii.2–5)

while on the other hand there is the now familiar 'sorrowing' sequence of Chapter xxxix consequent upon the 'donna gentile' moment of the text but turning now upon repentance as but a taking into self of the guilt apt otherwise to detain and ultimately to destroy the suffering spirit:

Contra questo avversario de la ragione si levoe un die, quasi ne l'ora de la nona, una forte imaginazione in me; che mi parve vedere questa gloriosa Beatrice con quelle vestimenta sanguigne co le quali apparve prima a li occhi miei; e pareami giovane in simile etade in quale io prima la vidi. Allora cominciai a pensare di lei. E ricordandomi di lei secondo l'ordine del tempo passato, lo mio cuore cominciò dolorosamente a pentere de lo desiderio a cui sì vilmente s'avea lasciato possedere alquanti die contra la costanzia de la ragione.

Over and against this adversary of reason, there arose within me one day, at about the ninth hour, a mighty vision in which, clothed in the crimson dress in which she had first appeared to me and seeming as young as when we first met, I beheld Beatrice in glory; whence I began thinking of her, and, recalling her thus in the order of time passing, I began

in my heart, with much sorrowing, to repent of the desire
to which, despite the steady insistence of reason, I had
delivered it.

(*Vita nova* xxxix. 1–2)

The pattern, then, is recognizably purgatorial, purgatory, in Dante's
sense of it, having everything to do with the soul-sorrowing
whereby, in and through the agony of it all, the pilgrim spirit seeks
to affirm self over self in the name and for the sake of its ultimate
homecoming, of the love-becoming to which it is called from
beforehand. And just as in the major work travail thus understood
shades off into triumph as that same pilgrim spirit lays hold at last
of the ecstatic substance of its properly human being-in-the-world,
so here in the *libello* the trauma of the 'donna gentile' episode is
resolved in an ascent of the spirit as rapturous as anything in Dante.
Everything, in other words, necessary for an at once more complete
and more seasoned statement of the matter in hand, of the paradisal
moment of human experience in its ideal resolution, is already there
in the little book; so, for example – though the inventory is in truth
infinitely expandable – the "sì come peregrino lo quale è fuori de la
sua patria, vi stae" ("there he stands like a pilgrim far from home")
of xli.5 for the "pur come pellegrin che tornar vuole" ("as with a
pilgrim anxious to return") of *Paradiso* I.5 1; the "che io non lo posso
intendere, cioè a dire che lo mio pensero sale ne la qualitade di costei
in grado che lo mio intelletto no lo puote comprendere" ("for I as
yet am unable to understand, my thought entering so far into her
essential nature that my intellect cannot as yet make sense of it") of
xli.6 for the "ch'io non lo 'ntesi, sì parlò profondo" ("I understood
her not, so profound were her words") of *Paradiso* XV.39; the "con
ciò sia cosa che lo nostro intelletto s'abbia a quelle benedette anime
sì come l'occhio debole a lo sole" ("for inasmuch as our mind is to
those blessed souls as a feeble eye is to the sun") of, again, xli.6 for
the "e fissi li occhi al sole oltre nostr' uso" ("I gazed into the sun in a
manner beyond our wont") of *Paradiso* I.54. This indeed, then, is the
paradisal moment of the *Vita nova*, the paradisal moment in Dante

always and everywhere being the moment of emergence, of, having known self in the far-offness of self, in its overwintering in a region of unlikeness, the spirit comes home at last to the fullness of its proper humanity – a notion contemplated for the moment by way of the courtly and neo-courtly categories of romance-vernacular versemaking, but, for all that, both fully formed and fully functional as a principle of self-understanding.

THREE

The *Convivio*

F AR-WANDERING AND FRIENDSHIP: THE courage of the
Convivio – feasting and faring well: a guide for the dispossessed –
crises of allegiance and a civic ontology.

FAR-WANDERING AND FRIENDSHIP: THE COURAGE OF THE *CONVIVIO*

The *Convivio* – the nothing if not magnanimous *Convivio* – is
the great work of Dante's middle period, of the years, that is to
say, leading up to and immediately following on from his exile in
the early part of 1302. And this, the catastrophe of exile, is worth
pausing over for a moment, for it is precisely the catastrophe of exile
that calls forth, quickens and sustains the courage of the *Convivio*
as, whatever else it is, an essay in self-recovery and self-affirmation,
in the building up of self in the wake of its tearing down. On the
one hand, then, and duly registered on the threshold of the text,
there is the humiliation and the indignity of it all, the predicament
of a proud spirit now displaced and present both to himself and to
those around him as but a wanderer on the face of the earth:

Ahi, piaciuto fosse al dispensatore de l'universo che la cagione
de la mia scusa mai non fosse stata! ché né altri contra me
avria fallato, né io sofferto avria pena ingiustamente, pena,
dico, d'essilio e di povertate. Poi che fu piacere de li cittadini
de la bellissima e famosissima figlia di Roma, Fiorenza, di
gittarmi fuori del suo dolce seno – nel quale nato e nutrito fui

in fino al colmo de la vita mia, e nel quale, con buona pace di quella, desidero con tutto lo cuore di riposare l'animo stancato e terminare lo tempo che m'è dato –, per le parti quasi tutte a le quali questa lingua si stende, peregrino, quasi mendicando, sono andato, mostrando contra mia voglia la piaga de la fortuna, che suole ingiustamente al piagato molte volte essere imputata. Veramente io sono stato legno sanza vela e sanza governo, portato a diversi porti e foci e liti dal vento secco che vapora la dolorosa povertade; e sono apparito a li occhi a molti che forseché per alcuna fama in altra forma m'aveano imaginato, nel conspetto de' quali non solamente mia persona invilio, ma di minor pregio si fece ogni opera, sì già fatta, come quella che fosse a fare.

Alas! Would that it had pleased the dispenser of the universe that the cause of my excuse might never have been; that others might neither have sinned against me, nor I have suffered punishment unjustly; the punishment, I say, of exile and poverty. Since it was the pleasure of the citizens of the most beautiful and the most famous daughter of Rome, Florence, to cast me out from her most sweet bosom (wherein I was born and nourished even to the height of my life, and in which, with her good will, I desire with all my heart to repose my weary soul, and to end the time that is given to me), I have gone through almost all the land in which this language lives – a pilgrim, almost a mendicant – showing forth against my will the wound of fortune, with which the ruined man is often unjustly reproached. Truly I have been a ship without a sail and without a rudder, borne to diverse ports and lands and shores by the dry wind that blows from doleful poverty; and I have appeared vile in the eyes of many, who perhaps through some report may have imagined me otherwise. In the sight of whom not only my person became vile, but each work, both completed and remaining yet to be done, was valued all the less.

(*Convivio* I.iii.3–5)

while on the other, and as registered now in the canzone *Tre
donne intorno al cor mi son venute* as one of the pinnacles of Dante's
achievement as a lyric poet, there is the ceaseless process of self-
interrogation in the forum of conscience, the to-and-fro conflict
of defiance and misgiving as each alike part and parcel of what it
means to be in exile:

> Tre donne intorno al cor mi son venute,
> e seggonsi di fore:
> ché dentro siede Amore,
> lo quale è in segnoria de la mia vita.
>   Tanto son belle e di tante vertute
> che 'l possente segnore,
> dico quel ch'è nel core,
> a pena del parlar di lor s'aita.
>   Ciascuna par dolente e sbigottita,
> come persona discacciata e stanca,
> cui tutta gente manca
> e cui vertute né beltà non vale.
> Tempo fu già nel quale,
> secondo il loro parlar, furon dilette;
> or sono a tutti in ira ed in non cale.
> Queste così solette
> venute son come a casa d'amico:
> ché sanno ben che dentro è quel ch'io dico.
> …
>   E io, che ascolto nel parlar divino
> consolarsi e dolersi
> così alti dispersi,
> l'essilio che m'è dato, onor mi tegno:
>   ché, se giudizio o forza di destino
> vuol pur che il mondo versi
> i bianchi fiori in persi,
> cader co' buoni è pur di lode degno.
>   E se non che de gli occhi miei 'l bel segno
> per lontananza m'è tolto dal viso,

che m'àve in foco miso,
lieve mi conterei ciò che m'è grave.
Ma questo foco m'àve
già consumato sì l'ossa e la polpa
che Morte al petto m'ha posto la chiave.
Onde, s'io ebbi colpa,
più lune ha volto il sol poi che fu spenta,
se colpa muore perché l'uom si penta.

Three women have come round my heart, and sit outside it, for within it is Love who holds sway over my life. They are so beautiful and of such dignity that the mighty Lord, I mean him in my heart, almost shrinks from speech with them. They each seem sorrowful and dismayed, like those driven from home and weary, abandoned by all, their virtue and beauty being of no avail. There was a time, to judge from their account, when they were loved, but now all regard them with hostility or indifference. All alone, then, they have come as to the house of a friend, for well they know that he of whom I speak is here … And I who listen to such noble exiles taking comfort and telling of their grief in divine speech, count as an honour the exile imposed on me; for if judgement or force of destiny does indeed desire that the world turn the white flowers into dark, it is still praiseworthy to fall with the good. And were it not that the fair goal of my eyes is removed by distance from my sight – and this has set me on fire – I would count as light that which weighs upon me. But that fire has already so consumed my bones and flesh that death has put his key to my breast. Whence even were I guilty, the sun has now circled for several moons since that was cancelled, if blame dies through repentance.

(*Tre donne intorno al cor mi son venute*, lines 1–18 and 73–90)

There can, therefore, be no sitting lightly to the agony of exile in Dante, to the restive humanity of one far from home. But – and this now is what matters – there is too the courage whereby, the agony of exile notwithstanding, he commits himself to a fresh shaping and substantiation of self as a poet and philosopher, to a fresh statement of the nature and finality of his passionate presence in the world. How so? Variously, to be sure, but by way not least of a fresh inclusivity, a fresh sense of the community as a whole – meaning by this the "many men and women in this language of ours burdened by domestic and civic care" – as astray with respect to its deep reasons, of what precisely it means fully and unequivocally *to be* in a certain set of socio-political, economic and linguistic circumstances. Now here we have as always to proceed with care, for we are as yet a good way off from the sublime sociology of the *Paradiso* with its sense of community as a matter, not merely of alongsidedness, but of indwelling, of one man's presence to another as but a structure of his very existence (the "intuare" and "inmiare" or "in-youing" and "in-meing" of the third canticle of the *Commedia*). But for all that, it is very definitely a matter now of solicitousness, of 'friendship' properly understood as a way of seeing, setting up and resolving both Dante's own humanity and that of the next man.

FEASTING AND FARING WELL: A GUIDE FOR THE DISPOSSESSED

This, then – this laying on of a banquet for the benefit of the socially and domestically disadvantaged (of a banquet amounting for the moment, however, to no more than a gathering up of whatever falls from the table of the wise) – is where Dante begins in the *Convivio*. Least as he is among the philosophers but loath to pass by on the other side, this feasting of his fellow man, he says, is but an act of compassion, of moral, certainly, but more than this of kindly concern:

> Ma però che ciascuno uomo a ciascuno uomo naturalmente è amico, e ciascuno amico si duole del difetto di colui ch'elli ama, coloro che a così alta mensa sono cibati non sanza misericordia sono inver di quelli che in bestiale pastura veggiono erba e ghiande sen gire mangiando. E acciò che misericordia è madre

di beneficio, sempre liberalmente coloro che sanno porgono de la loro buona ricchezza a li veri poveri, e sono quasi fonte vivo, de la cui acqua si refrigera la naturale sete che di sopra è nominata. E io adunque, che non seggio a la beata mensa, ma, fuggito de la pastura del vulgo, a' piedi di coloro che seggiono ricolgo di quello che da loro cade, e conosco la misera vita di quelli che dietro m'ho lasciati, per la dolcezza ch'io sento in quello che a poco a poco ricolgo, misericordievolmente mosso, non me dimenticando, per li miseri alcuna cosa ho riservata, la quale a li occhi loro, già è più tempo, ho dimostrata; e in ciò li ho fatti maggiormente vogliosi.

But since every man is by nature a friend of every other man, and every man is grieved by any lack in the one he loves, those who are fed at such an exalted table are not without compassion towards those they see wandering in lowly pastures feeding on grass and acorns. And since compassion is the mother of action, those in possession of understanding always give generously from their bounty to those genuinely in need, for they are like a living fountain whose waters slake the natural thirst of which I spoke a moment ago. I, therefore, who do not myself sit at the blessed table, but rather, having fled the pasture of the commonalty, take my place at the feet of those who are so seated, gathering up as I do so whatever falls from it, acknowledge the wretched state of those I have left behind; and, sensitive to the sweetness of what little I have been able to save and moved by compassion, I have (albeit without forgetting myself) set aside something for those poor folk – something for which, in that I placed it before them quite a while ago now, they are all the more eager.

(*Convivio* I.i.8–10)

– lines to which, as bearing both on the composition and on the gendering of Dante's chosen readership in the *Convivio*, we may add these from later in the book:

... e questi nobili sono principi, baroni, cavalieri, e molt'altra nobile gente, non solamente maschi ma femmine, che sono molti e molte in questa lingua, volgari, e non litterati.

... and these noble folk comprise princes, barons, knights and many noble souls to boot, men and women alike and all of them, numerous as they are, vernacular rather than Latinate.

(*Convivio* I.ix.5)

And it is this concern for the well-being of the next man, or at any rate of the next man as detained by domestic and civic responsibility, that determines the main business of this first book of the *Convivio*, namely its opting for the vernacular rather than for Latin as best suited to the matter in hand. True, the choice requires some justification, Latin, from the point of view of its stable complexion, of its expressive power and of its long since celebrated beauty, being on the face of it the language of choice. All this, therefore, in Chapter v as preliminary in respect of everything coming next by way of Dante's *apologia pro lingua sua* in the *Convivio* and indeed of what amounts in just about the same breath to his *volte-face* hereabouts; for by the time we reach Chapter x he has changed his mind. If, then, in respect of its permanence Latin remains still the nobler of the two languages, in respect of its power fully and sufficiently to articulate the idea and of its gentle concatenation of sound and syntax the vernacular is quite the equal of 'grammar'. Neither expressively, then, nor aesthetically is there anything to choose between them, the twofold sweetness and sinuousness of the vernacular line being matched only by its capacity to ravish the spirit:

Ché per questo comento la gran bontade del volgare di sì [si vedrà]; però che si vedrà la sua vertù, sì com'è per esso altissimi e novissimi concetti convenevolmente, sufficientemente e acconciamente, quasi come per esso latino, manifestare; [la quale non si potea bene manifestare] ne le cose rimate, per le accidentali adornezze che quivi sono connesse, cioè la rima e lo ri[ti]mo e lo numero regolato; sì come non si può bene manifestare la bellezza d'una donna, quando li adornamenti de l'azzimare e de le vestimenta la fanno più ammirare che essa medesima. Onde chi vuole ben giudicare d'una donna, guardi quella quando solo sua naturale bellezza si sta con lei, da tutto accidentale adornamento discompagnata; sì come sarà questo comento, nel quale si vedrà l'agevolezza de le sue sillabe, le proprietadi de le sue co[stru]zioni e le soavi orazioni che di lui si fanno, le quali chi bene agguarderà, vedrà essere piene di dolcissima e d'amabilissima bellezza.

By way, then, of this commentary, the great goodness of the Italian vernacular will become apparent; for in it will be seen the power it has to express the most sublime and novel ideas as fittingly, as fully and as elegantly as Latin itself – a power that cannot be shown forth so readily in verse on account of the incidental embellishment pertaining to it (namely rhyme and rhythm), any more, in fact, than can the beauty of a woman when the trappings of her finery and attire draw more attention than she herself (which is why whoever wishes properly to judge of a woman should irrespective of accidental adornment look upon her in her natural beauty). That, then, is how this commentary will appear, for everywhere apparent will be the gracious movement of its syllables, the elegance of its periods and the sweet discourse fashioned from it, which things, for those caring to look closely into the matter, will have about them both the sweetest and the loveliest beauty.

(*Convivio* I.x.12–13)

But that, where the vernacular is concerned, is not all, for the *Convivio* thus conceived, as a feast laid on by Dante for an otherwise busy lay intelligentsia, is a gift, and a gift is a gift only in the degree to which it is liberally conceived, joyfully given and genuinely useful to the recipient, short of which it is a mere bequest or transaction. This, then, from the point of view of Dante's general undertaking in the *Convivio*, of his laying on a banquet for the spiritually disenfranchised, is the basis of his linguistic preference in the book; no vernacular, no generosity, simply an empty and to that extent meaningless gesture in respect of those both seeking and deserving something better:

> Tornando dunque al principale proposito, dico che manifestamente si può vedere come lo latino averebbe a pochi dato lo suo beneficio, ma lo volgare servirà veramente a molti. Ché la bontà de l'animo, la quale questo servigio attende, è in coloro che per malvagia disusanza del mondo hanno lasciata la litteratura a coloro che l'hanno fatta di donna meretrice; e questi nobili sono principi, baroni, cavalieri, e molt'altra nobile gente, non solamente maschi ma femmine, che sono molti e molte in questa lingua, volgari, e non litterati.

> To return, then, to my main theme, it is, I maintain, perfectly plain to see how Latin would have benefited very few, whereas the vernacular will serve the interests of many; for excellence of mind is to be found only in those who, having alas neglected these things by reason of their busyness in the world, have abandoned letters only to those making a harlot of them – in those many worthy princes, barons, knights, including men and women alike, who, having the vernacular but no Latin, abound in this language of ours.

> (*Convivio* I.ix.4–5)

In truth, however, the argument here runs a good deal deeper than this, for the greatest beneficiary of the vernacular has been, Dante thinks, he himself, at which point the love-intensity of this whole question of language, not to say the deep vernacularity of his entire being and doing as a poet and philosopher, moves clearly into view. First, then, we have the moment of recognition, the moment in which, turning away for an instant from his chosen clientele in the book to put on record his own situation, he testifies to the indispensability of the vernacular to his own coming about both in the flesh and in the spirit – in the flesh by way of the vernacular as the in-and-through-which of his parents' intercourse (the "concorso a la mia generazione" moment of the argument), and in the spirit by way of that same vernacular as his readying for still higher things, for the blessings of a Latin culture conducive not simply to his being but to his being well as a creature of moral and intellectual awareness:

Questo mio volgare fu congiugnitore de li miei generanti, che con esso parlavano, sì come 'l fuoco è disponitore del ferro al fabbro che fa lo coltello; per che manifesto è lui essere concorso a la mia generazione, e così essere alcuna cagione del mio essere. Ancora, questo mio volgare fu introduttore di me ne la via di scienza, che è ultima perfezione, in quanto con esso io entrai ne lo latino e con esso mi fu mostrato: lo quale latino poi mi fu via a più innanzi andare. E così è palese, e per me conosciuto, esso essere stato a me grandissimo benefattore.

Just like the fire that readies the iron for the smith to make a knife, this vernacular of mine, being the language my parents spoke, brought them together, it being clear, therefore, that it was implicated in my own coming about, among the causes of my being. Moreover, in that with its help I made a start in Latin and was aided in my understanding of it, this same vernacular set me on the road to knowledge as the greatest perfection, Latin being that whereby I was able to make further progress. It is clear, therefore – and this I gladly acknowledge – that this my vernacular has been my most wonderful benefactor.

(*Convivio* I.xiii.4–5)

But then, and no less resplendently, comes the 'love-intensity' moment of the argument, the moment in which, having confirmed the length, the breadth, the height and the depth of his companionship with the vernacular, Dante commits himself yet again to its welfare, his entire discourse hereabouts culminating in something close to a giving and receiving of vows:

Anche, è stato meco d'uno medesimo studio, e ciò posso così mostrare. Ciascuna cosa studia naturalmente a la sua conservazione; onde, se lo volgare per sé studiare potesse, studierebbe a quella; e quella sarebbe, acconciare sé a più stabilitade, e più stabilitade non potrebbe avere che in legar sé con numero e con rime. E questo medesimo studio è stato mio, sì come tanto è palese che non dimanda testimonianza. Per che uno medesimo studio è stato lo suo e 'l mio; per che di questa concordia l'amistà è confermata e accresciuta. Anche c'è stata la benivolenza de la consuetudine, ché dal principio de la mia vita ho avuta con esso benivolenza e conversazione, e usato quello diliberando, interpetrando e questionando. Per che, se l'amistà s'accresce per la consuetudine, sì come sensibilmente appare, manifesto è che essa in me massimamente è cresciuta, che sono con esso volgare tutto mio tempo usato. E così si vede essere a questa amistà concorse tutte le cagioni generative e accrescitive de l'amistade; per che si conchiude che non solamente amore, ma perfettissimo amore sia quello ch'io a lui debbo avere e ho.

Further, and as I shall now demonstrate, we have together sought out but one and the same goal; for everything naturally seeks to preserve its own being. If, then, the vernacular were itself able to seek out an end, that indeed is what it would seek – to wit, the still greater stability of rhythm and rhyme as that whereby it is properly bound up. This, as something requiring no further proof, is the very goal I have set myself. We both of us, then, have sought out the same thing, this common commitment of ours being by way of a firm and ever developing friendship. And then there has been the longstanding good will of it all, I, from my earliest days, having enjoyed with the vernacular a tender companionship, calling upon it for my every deliberation, my every judgement in point of meaning and my every enquiry after the truth. So if as most certainly seems to be the case friendship is deepened by familiarity, then this, manifestly and indeed supremely, has been true for me as having had a constant concern for this language of ours. Plainly, then, everything making for friendship be it by way of its quickening or of its nurturing has been at work here too, whence it follows that mine, for the vernacular, is a matter, not simply of love, but of the most perfect love, this being but what I owe and what I indeed profess.

(*Convivio* I.xiii.6–10)

With what in this sense constitutes a love-profession as intimate as it is intense it only remains to state afresh the overall purpose of the *Convivio*, namely a feeding of the five thousand designed to bring them on in the way of properly human happiness, and this by way of the vernacular as but a new light to lighten the gentiles:

Così rivolgendo li occhi a dietro, e raccogliendo le ragioni prenotate, puotesi vedere questo pane, col quale si deono mangiare le infrascritte canzoni, essere sufficientemente purgato da le macule, e da l'essere di biado; per che tempo è d'intendere a ministrare le vivande. Questo sarà quello pane orzato del quale si satolleranno migliaia, e a me ne soperchieranno le sporte piene. Questo sarà luce nuova, sole nuovo, lo quale surgerà là dove l'usato tramonterà, e darà lume a coloro che sono in tenebre e in oscuritade, per lo usato sole che a loro non luce.

Looking back, then, over all that has been said, and gathering up the threads of the argument so far, it is clear that this bread, with which the following canzoni should be eaten, has been sufficiently purged of any blemish and excused for being but of barley. So now, then, it is time to think about serving the courses themselves, this commentary constituting the barley bread whereby – with many a basketful besides remaining to me – thousands will be satisfied. This will be a new light, a new sun rising where the old has set, a light to enlighten the darkling and overshadowed, the sun of old no longer shining upon them.

(*Convivio* I.xiii.11–12)

With this, then, Dante is ready to move on to what in Books II and III amounts to a preparation for the main course of his banquet, to a hymn to philosophy as but the love of wisdom first and foremost in God himself, this, however, being a love tending to recreate in its own likeness every instance of properly human loving, this in turn being the ground and guarantee of man's greatest happiness as man. Before getting under way, however, there is a small question of methodology to address and as far as may be to resolve; for the *Convivio*, like the *Vita nova*, takes the form of a commentary on a number of Dante's own poems as, so to speak, the meat of his discourse, poems that, being in the case of the first two at any rate allegorical in kind, require of writer and reader alike a certain exegetical sophistication. In fact, what could have turned out to be a rather tricky question, there being as Dante says two different kinds of allegory (that of the poets with its simple *either/or* structure, its simple saying of one thing and meaning something else, and that of the theologians with its more complex *both/and* structure, its involving different levels of meaning at one and the same time), is settled by way of his opting in principle for the former rather than the latter, any of the more esoteric or hidden meanings of the text being touched upon as and when:

> Veramenti li teologi questo senso prendono altrimenti che li poeti; ma però che mia intenzione è qui lo modo de li poeti seguitare, prendo lo senso allegorico secondo che per li poeti è usato … Io adunque, per queste ragioni, tuttavia sopra ciascuna canzone ragionerò prima la litterale sentenza, e appresso di quella ragionerò la sua allegoria, cioè la nascosa veritade; e talvolta de li altri sensi toccherò incidentemente, come a luogo e a tempo si converrà.

> Theologians, to be sure, understand this allegorical sense otherwise than the poets, but since I purpose here to follow the way of the poets I shall take it in the sense that they do … For these reasons, then, I, in discussing each canzone, will start out from its literal meaning, coming only then to its allegorical meaning or hidden truth, touching only occasionally on the other senses as time and place require.

> (*Convivio* II.i.4 and 15)

With this, then, the way is clear for an account of the first poem chosen for commentary, the canzone *Voi che 'ntendendo il terzo ciel movete*, a poem having to do in its literal sense with the nothing if not painful triumph of one love over another, of – contrary now to the substance and the solution of the *Vita nova* – the triumph of the gracious lady of the casement over Beatrice as but the "gloriosa donna de la mia mente", the glorious lady of his mind. Contemplating afresh, therefore, the trauma at the centre of his existence, Dante addresses the 'movers of the third heaven' as those he holds to be accountable for it:

> Voi che 'ntendendo il terzo ciel movete,
> udite il ragionar ch'è nel mio core,
> ch'io nol so dire altrui, sì mi par novo.
>   El ciel che segue lo vostro valore,
> gentili creature che voi sete,
> mi tragge ne lo stato ov'io mi trovo.
>   Onde 'l parlar de la vita ch'io provo
> par che si drizzi degnamente a vui:
> però vi priego che lo mi 'ntendiate.
> Io vi dirò del cor la novitate
> come l'anima trista piange in lui,
> e come un spirto contra lei favella,
> che vien pe' raggi de la vostra stella.
>
>   Suol esser vita de lo cor dolente
> un soave penser, che se ne gia
> molte fiate a' pie' del nostro Sire,
>   ove una donna gloriar vedia,
> di cui parlava me sì dolcemente
> che l'anima dicea: "Io men vo' gire".
>   Or apparisce chi lo fa fuggire
> e segnoreggia me di tal virtute,
> che 'l cor ne trema che di fuori appare.
> Questi mi face una donna guardare,
> e dice: "Chi veder vuol la salute,

faccia che li occhi d'esta donna miri,
sed e' non teme angoscia di sospiri".

O you who by understanding move the third heaven, hear the reasoning within my heart, for so strange is it to me that of it I can speak to none other. The heaven moving at your behest, noble creatures that you are, draws me into my present state, which is why speaking of the life I am living is properly addressed to you, and thus I crave your attention. Of the strange state of my heart I shall tell you, of how there my sad soul weeps and of how a spirit coming in the rays of your star enters into contention with her. The life of my sorrowing heart used to be a gracious thought making its way often to the feet of our Lord, where, seeing a lady in glory of whom it would speak so sweetly my soul would declare: "I too wish to go there." But now there appears one putting it to flight, one who lords it over me with such power that the trembling of my heart is plain for all to see. This same one constrains me to look at a woman, saying the while: "Provided only that he shrink not from grievous sighing, let him who would know salvation gaze into the eyes of this lady."

(*Voi che 'ntendendo il terzo ciel movete*, lines 1–26)

But who, exactly, are these 'movers of the third heaven' that they should be thus consulted upon a matter falling within their remit? The answer, Dante thinks, calls for a little cosmology. First, then – and it is, of course, a question here of the geocentricity of it all – come the circling spheres of the observable universe, or, more exactly, the heavenly bodies attached to those spheres: the Moon, Mercury, Venus, the Sun, Mars, Jupiter and Saturn, with the earth nestling foetus-like in the centre. Beyond these are the firmament comprising those stars so far away that they appear to be stationary, the *primum mobile* responsible for imparting movement to the *machina mundi* as a whole, and the Empyrean, co-extensive and consubstantial with the divine mind as the all-circumscribing but uncircumscribed whereabouts of it all. Thus the created world as a whole is contained within the pure, primordial and limitless spirituality of the *Protonoé* or First Mind where according to the infallible testimony of the Church the elect live out into all eternity their blessed existence. The key passage, hymnic in its sense of the sublimity of it all, runs as follows:

> Ed è l'ordine del sito questo, che lo primo che numerano è quello dove è la Luna; lo secondo è quello dov'è Mercurio; lo terzo è quello dov'è Venere; lo quarto è quello dove è lo Sole; lo quinto è quello di Marte; lo sesto è quello di Giove; lo settimo è quello di Saturno; l'ottavo è quello de le Stelle; lo nono è quello che non è sensibile se non per questo movimento che è detto di sopra, lo quale chiamano molti Cristallino, cioè diafano, o vero tutto trasparente. Veramente, fuori di tutti questi, li cattolici pongono lo cielo Empireo, che è a dire cielo di fiamma o vero luminoso; e pongono esso essere immobile per avere in sé, secondo ciascuna parte, ciò che la sua materia vuole. E questo è cagione al Primo Mobile per avere velocissimo movimento; ché per lo ferventissimo appetito ch'è in ciascuna parte di quello nono cielo, che è immediato a quello, d'essere congiunta con ciascuna parte di quello divinissimo ciel quieto, in quello si rivolve con tanto desiderio, che la sua velocitade è quasi incomprensibile. E quieto e pacifico è lo luogo di quella somma Deitade che sola [sé] compiutamente vede. Questo loco è di spiriti beati, secondo che la Santa Chiesa vuole, che non può dire menzogna; e Aristotile pare ciò sentire, a chi bene lo 'ntende, nel primo De Celo et Mundo. Questo è lo soprano edificio del mondo, nel quale tutto lo mondo s'inchiude, e di fuori dal quale nulla è; ed esso non è in luogo ma formato fu solo ne la prima Mente, la quale li Greci dicono Protonoè. Questa è quella magnificenza, de la quale parlò il Salmista, quando dice a Dio: "Levata è la magnificenza tua sopra li cieli". E così ricogliendo ciò che ragionato è, pare che diece cieli siano, de li quali quello di Venere sia lo terzo, del quale si fa menzione in quella parte che mostrare intendo.

The heavens are arranged thus, the first of their number being that of the Moon; the second, Mercury; the third, Venus; the fourth, the Sun; the fifth, Mars; the sixth Jupiter; the seventh, Saturn; and the eighth, that of the fixed stars. The ninth, which is not perceptible to the senses other than by way of the movement mentioned above, is called by many – diaphanous or totally transparent as it is – the Crystalline. Beyond these, however, Catholics locate the Empyrean, meaning the heaven of flame or, more exactly of light, which heaven, possessing as it does in its every part the perfection required by its matter, they hold to be motionless. That is why the *primum mobile* is so incredibly swift, for since in that ninth sphere there burns an ardent desire to be united in its every part with every part of that most divine heaven, it revolves within that heaven with a yearning so intense that its speed is beyond all understanding. Perfectly at peace, by contrast, is the dwelling place of the Godhead on high, of the One who alone fully sees himself. Indeed according to the Church, which bears no false witness, and with whom Aristotle, rightly understood, appears in the first book of the *De celo et mundo* to agree, this is the dwelling place of the blessed. It is the sovereign structure of the universe, by which the whole universe is contained and beyond which there is nothing at all. It is not itself in space, but rather was fashioned within the primal mind, within, as the Greeks call it, the *Protonoé*. It is the splendour of which the Psalmist spoke when, addressing God, he said: "Your splendour is exalted above the heavens." And so to sum up in respect of what we have said so far, it is clear that there are ten heavens, of which the heaven of Venus mentioned in that section of the canzone which I now intend to expound is the third.

(*Convivio* II.iii.7–12)

– lines to which, as homing in now on the so-called 'movers' of the heavenly bodies thus understood, we may add these from Book III with their sense of those movers as but the Intelligences associated with those same heavenly bodies and responsible for the modulation here below of the idea pure and simple as present to the divine mind:

E qui è da sapere che ciascuno Intelletto di sopra, secondo ch'è scritto nel libro de le Cagioni, conosce quello che è sopra sé e quello che è sotto sé. Conosce adunque Iddio sì come sua cagione, conosce quello che è sotto sé sì come suo effetto; e però che Dio è universalissima cagione di tutte le cose, conoscendo lui, tutte le cose conosce in sé, secondo lo modo de la Intelligenza. Per che tutte le Intelligenze conoscono la forma umana, in quanto ella è per intenzione regolata ne la divina mente; e massimamente conoscono quella le Intelligenze motrici, però che sono spezialissime cagioni di quella e d'ogni forma generale, e conoscono quella perfettissima, tanto quanto essere puote, sì come loro regola ed essemplo. E se essa umana forma, essemplata e individuata, non è perfetta, non è manco de lo detto essemplo, ma de la materia la quale individua. Però quando dico: *Ogni Intelletto di là su la mira*, non voglio altro dire se non ch'ella è così fatta come l'essemplo intenzionale che de la umana essenzia è ne la divina mente e, per quella, in tutte l'altre, massimamente in quelle menti angeliche che fabbricano col cielo queste cose di qua giuso.

It is important here to appreciate that, as set out in the *Book of Causes*, each Intellect above has an understanding of what is higher and of what is lower than itself. So each knows God as its cause and what is lower than itself as its effect; and since God is the most universal cause of all things, in knowing him it knows all things, and this with the kind of knowledge proper to an Intelligence. Consequently, all the Intelligences know the human form as present intentionally to the divine mind. It is known especially to the Intelligences responsible for movement, since they in particular are the cause both of the human form and of form generally. As present to them, moreover, both as norm and as exemplar, they know it in its most perfect state, in all that it has it in itself to be. If, therefore, this human form, once actualized in this or that positive instance, is less than perfect, this is down not to any deficiency in the aforesaid exemplar but to the matter responsible for its individuation. When, therefore, I say that *Every Intellect on high looks upon her* what I have in mind is that she herself constitutes the ideal form of mankind as present to the divine mind, and, by way of this, to every other mind including above all the angelic minds responsible by means of the heavens for the fashioning of things here below.

(Convivio III.vi.4–6)

as well as, for the record (but in truth for their exquisite formulation of an exquisite notion), these from the second canto of the *Paradiso* relative once again to the step-by-step implementation of the idea by the Intelligences as, here too, receiving from above and fashioning below:

> Dentro dal ciel de la divina pace
> si gira un corpo ne la cui virtute
> l'esser di tutto suo contento giace.
> 　Lo ciel seguente, c'ha tante vedute,
> quell' esser parte per diverse essenze,
> da lui distratte e da lui contenute.
> 　Li altri giron per varie differenze
> le distinzion che dentro da sé hanno
> dispongono a lor fini e lor semenze.
> 　Questi organi del mondo così vanno,
> come tu vedi omai, di grado in grado,
> che di sù prendono e di sotto fanno.

Within the heaven of divine peace spins a body in the might of which lies the being of everything it contains. The next heaven, with its many lights, distributes that being instance by instance, those instances being at once comprehended by and distinct from it. The remaining spheres, variously differentiated, order the now distinct forms they contain to their proper end and seminal substance. So it is that, as you can now see, these organs of the universe proceed step by step to receive from above and to fashion below.

(*Paradiso* II.112–23)

If, then, the Intelligences of whom the poet speaks are those who, contemplating the idea as present to the divine mind, preside over its realization in time and space, then the movers of the third heaven in particular – the heaven of Venus – are those he seeks now to address. As plaintiff in an affair of the heart he has taken his case to the top.

But the canzone *Voi che 'ntendendo il terzo ciel movete* is allegorical, its literal sense being but a beautiful lie (the "bella menzogna" of II.i.3), a gracious mantle in respect of its true meaning. Strictly, then, the poem has to do with Dante's preoccupation, not, in fact, with the compassionate lady of the casement, but with "the most beautiful and virtuous daughter of the Emperor of the Universe, known to Pythagoras as Philosophy" (the "bellissima e onestissima figlia de lo imperadore de lo universo, a la quale Pittagora pose nome Filosofia" of II.xv.12), with the muse and mistress, that is to say, of those speculative spirits, ancient and modern alike, from whom he drew comfort in the moment of his bereavement. How so? By way, he explains, of the likeness or analogy that may be said to exist (*a*) between the stars and the sciences generally (where by the term 'sciences' we mean the seven disciplines of the *trivium* and the *quadrivium*, the three Peripatetic sciences of physics, metaphysics and ethics, and the properly Christian science of theology), and (*b*) between this or that star and this or that science in particular. As far, then, as the first of these things is concerned we may say this, that just as the stars in general move about a fixed point, variously irradiating as they do so the world here below, so also do the sciences in general, each alike, turning as it does about its own still centre of concern, serving to irradiate the mind. As far, by contrast, as the second of them is concerned we may say this, that there is a distinct and thus discernible likeness between each of the heavens and each of the sciences in turn; so, for example, the Moon and the science of grammar, each alike changeable with the passage of time; or Mercury and the science of logic or dialectic, each alike as compact as it is powerful; or the Sun and arithmetic, each alike shedding light on the shape and structure of things; or Mars and music, each alike tending to lay hold of and to possess the spirit in its entirety; or Jupiter and geometry, each alike notable for its radiant aspect; or Saturn and astronomy, the most elevated and the stateliest of the stars and of the sciences respectively. And what applies to those stars in, so to speak, our vicinity and to the sciences of the *trivium* and *quadrivium* applies also to the firmament, the *primum mobile* and to the Peripatetic sciences of physics, metaphysics and ethics decisive for the shape and substance of scholastic consciousness generally; thus the firmament, in its presence to us under the aspect both of the seen and of the unseen, resembles physics and metaphysics as turning respectively on the empirical and on the speculative encounter, while the Crystalline or *primum mobile* as the origin in the universe of all movement resembles ethics as the structural or organizational science *par excellence* in human affairs, as that whereby all that we seek to be and to do in this world as creatures of moral determination is subject to proper regulation. And then finally there is the Empyrean, all of a piece with theology in its stillness and, by way of the certainty it affords as but the encompassing, in its power to assuage the troubled spirit.

This then, Dante explains, is where we must look for his meaning in *Voi che 'ntendendo il terzo ciel movete*, Venus and the Intelligences by which it is moved being none other than rhetoric and the sweet voice thereof as represented in the moment of his bereavement by Boethius on consolation and by Cicero on friendship, and the compassionate lady of the casement none other than Philosophy herself as the inspiration of all those seeking out the ways and means of properly human happiness. Little wonder, therefore, that he should surrender! For to stand in the company of My Lady Philosophy and to look into her eyes as but the sweet demonstration of the truth she embodies is to know self in the bliss of unclouded intellection:

Ove si vuole sapere che questa donna è la Filosofia; la quale veramente è donna piena di dolcezza, ornata d'onestade, mirabile di savere, gloriosa di libertade, sì come nel terzo trattato, dove la sua nobilitade si tratterà, fia manifesto. E là dove dice: *Chi veder vuol la salute, Faccia che li occhi d'esta donna miri*, li occhi di questa donna sono le sue demonstrazioni le quali, dritte ne li occhi de lo 'ntelletto, innamorano l'anima, liberata da le con[tra]dizioni. O dolcissimi e ineffabili sembianti, e rubatori subitani de la mente umana, che ne le mostrazioni de li occhi de la Filosofia apparite, quando essa con li suoi drudi ragiona! Veramente in voi è la salute, per la quale si fa beato chi vi guarda, e salvo da la morte de la ignoranza e da li vizii.

What we need to understand, then, is that the lady in question is Philosophy, in truth (and as we shall make clear in the next part of the book focusing on her nobility), a woman tender beyond words, graciously adorned, wondrous in her wisdom, and resplendent in her freedom. Thus where it says *Who would see salvation, let him look into the eyes of this woman*, her eyes are understood to be her power to persuade – eyes which, once trained upon those of the mind, straightaway enamour the soul in its freedom now from its every difficulty along the way. O glances most sweet and ineffable, which, in the moment you appear in madonna's eyes as she discourses with those she most cherishes, take possession of the human mind! Truly all blessedness is in you, those looking upon you knowing perfect bliss, nay salvation from the death of ignorance and error.

(*Convivio* II.xv.3–4)

To gaze, then, if only for an instant upon the face of the "donna gentile" as but a way of seeing and celebrating the love of wisdom all of a piece with the Godhead is to know self in the rapturous substance of self, in the sheer exhilaration thereof, all of which, as we pass from Book II of the *Convivio* to Book III, encourages Dante to do what Dante does best, which is to dwell neither for the first time nor for the last (*a*) on the notion of what love, as love, actually is, and (*b*) on the idea of love as yet again a principle of transfiguration, as, here in the *Convivio*, that whereby the individual is made over again in the likeness of his or her maker. Love, then, properly understood, is nothing other than a reaching out on the part of the one who loves for communion with the object of that love, a reaching out variously conditioned, to be sure, by nature and circumstance but always and everywhere urgent – not to say athletic (Dante's "corre tosto e tardi") – in kind:

> Amore, veramente pigliando e sottilmente considerando, non è altro che unimento spirituale de l'anima e de la cosa amata; nel quale unimento di propia sua natura l'anima corre tosto e tardi, secondo che è libera o impedita.

> Love, properly and carefully considered, is nothing other than the spiritual union of the soul and the object of its affection, which union the soul, in keeping with its proper nature, hastens be it swiftly or slowly to enjoy according to the degree or otherwise of its freedom.

> (*Convivio* III.ii.3)

But that same love, Dante goes on, is a complex business, for man as man reaches out for the object of his affection, not merely morally and intellectually, but minerally, vegetatively and sensitively, after the manner, that is to say, not simply of the angels, but of the stones beneath his feet, of the plants delighting in the sun and the soil as the in-and-through-which of their well-being, and of the beasts of the field rejoicing as they do one in the company of another. True, the love most proper to man is the love of the rational soul whereby he reaches out for whatsoever things are pure, whatsoever things are lovely and whatsoever things are of good report, but for all that, he loves and loves legitimately in all these ways:

> Onde è da sapere che ciascuna cosa, come detto è di sopra, per la ragione di sopra mostrata ha 'l suo speziale amore. Come le corpora simplici hanno amore naturato in sé a lo luogo proprio, e però la terra sempre discende al centro; lo fuoco ha [amore a] la circunferenza di sopra, lungo lo cielo de la

luna, e però sempre sale a quello. Le corpora composte prima, sì come sono le minere, hanno amore a lo luogo dove la loro generazione è ordinata, e in quello crescono e acquistano vigore e potenza; onde vedemo la calamita sempre da la parte de la sua generazione ricevere vertù. Le piante, che sono prima animate, hanno amore a certo luogo più manifestamente, secondo che la complessione richiede; e però vedemo certe piante lungo l'acque quasi c[ontent]arsi, e certe sopra li gioghi de le montagne, e certe ne le piagge e dappiè monti; le quali se si transmutano, o muoiono del tutto o vivono quasi triste, disgiunte dal loro amico. Li animali bruti hanno più manifesto amore non solamente a li luoghi, ma l'uno l'altro vedemo amare. Li uomini hanno loro proprio amore a le perfette e oneste cose. E però che l'uomo, avvegna che una sola sustanza sia, tuttavia [la] forma, per la sua nobilitade, ha in sé e la natura [d'ognuna di] queste cose, tutti questi amori puote avere e tutti li ha.

What, then, we need to understand is this, that, for the reason shown above, everything has its own proper love. Just as simple bodies have within them a natural love for their proper place, which is why earth is always drawn to its centre, and just as fire has a natural love for the sphere above us bordering that of the Moon, and so always rises towards it, so the primary compound bodies, the minerals, have a love for the place where they are created, and where they grow and whence they derive vigour and energy; thus we find that a magnet always acquires its power from the place whence it comes. Plants, which are the primary form of animate being, have a clear preference for certain places, according to their needs; so some plants we see to be at their happiest alongside water, while others thrive on high peaks or else on slopes or in the foothills, all of which either perish or linger on sadly if uprooted and parted from their friends. Brute animals have an even more obvious love, not only for particular places, but for one another. Human beings too have their proper love, in this case for all things good and praiseworthy. And since man, though but one in substance, comprehends by way of the nobility of his form all these things, he can and does love in all these ways.

(*Convivio* III.iii.2–5)

Now, however, a discourse as yet merely preliminary in respect of the *what* and the *how* of properly human loving stands to be developed, and indeed *is* developed, in terms of something more properly sublime; for to love well, Dante thinks, is to be drawn into the very substance of the beloved there to be made conformable to it, to rediscover self in the now revised dimensionality of self – all of which means that to know and to love the Godhead as but coeval and consubstantial with his own love of wisdom is to be drawn into the very likeness thereof, knowing self in the very likeness thereof being in turn to rejoice *sub specie aeternitatis* in the love-abundance of it all. Taking again, then – but pausing over what amounts now to its systematic statement – the notion of the Godhead as nothing other than the love of wisdom proper to it as of the essence (the divine nature suffering no addition), we have these lines from III.xii:

Ché se a memoria si reduce ciò che detto è di sopra, filosofia è uno amoroso uso di sapienza, lo quale massimamente è in Dio, però che in lui è somma sapienza e sommo amore e sommo atto; che non può essere altrove, se non in quanto da esso procede. È adunque la divina filosofia de la divina essenza, però che in esso non può essere cosa a la sua essenzia aggiunta; ed è nobilissima, però che nobilissima è la essenzia divina; ed è in lui per modo perfetto e vero, quasi per etterno matrimonio.

For if we call to mind what was said above, philosophy is but a loving exercise of wisdom, something that – since in him are supreme wisdom, supreme love and supreme act – exists above all in God, and indeed is nowhere else to be found other than insofar as it proceeds from him. Given, then, that the divine essence admits of no addition, divine philosophy is of that essence, the surpassing nobility of the one being the surpassing nobility of the other. In him it subsists both perfectly and truly, by way, so to speak, of eternal wedlock.

(*Convivio* III.xii.12–13)

while as following on from this and as Dante's point of arrival in the third book of the *Convivio* we have these from III.xiv bearing upon the 'assimilative' component of his discourse, his nothing if not radiant sense of how it is that in loving thus the lover is fashioned afresh in the likeness of his maker, thereafter and for evermore knowing himself in the blessed transformation of self:

> Onde in questo verso che seguentemente comincia: *In lei discende la virtù divina*, io intendo commendare l'amore, che è parte de la filosofia. Ove è da sapere che discender la virtude d'una cosa in altra non è altro che ridurre quella in sua similitudine, sì come ne li agenti naturali vedemo manifestamente; che, discendendo la loro virtù ne le pazienti cose, recano quelle a loro similitudine, tanto quanto possibili sono a venire ad essa. Onde vedemo lo sole che, discendendo lo raggio suo qua giù, reduce le cose a sua similitudine di lume, quanto esse per loro disposizione possono da la [sua] virtude lume ricevere. Così dico che Dio questo amore a sua similitudine reduce, quanto esso è possibile a lui assimigliarsi ... E ciò si può fare manifesto massimamente in ciò, che sì come lo divino amore è tutto etterno, così conviene che sia etterno lo suo obietto di necessitate, sì che etterne cose siano quelle che esso ama. E così face questo amore amare; ché la sapienza, ne la quale questo amore fere, etterna è.

And so in the stanza immediately following – the one beginning *Divine power descends into her* – my purpose is to commend love as but part of philosophy. What, then, we need to understand here is this, that to speak of the power of one thing descending into another is to speak of its fashioning that thing in its own likeness, for that, plainly, is the way things behave in the world; when their power descends into objects patient of this they draw those objects into their own likeness at any rate to the extent that those objects are capable thereof. Whence, for example, we see the sun's rays shed upon things here below and, to the extent, at least, that those things are fitted by nature for it, transforming them by way of the light falling upon them and duly received by them. What I am saying, then, is that insofar as its nature permits, God draws this love into a likeness of himself ... and this is evident above all in that, just as divine love is itself all eternal, so of necessity is the object of that love, such that everything God loves is eternal. And so he causes this love to love, the wisdom upon which his love bears being itself eternal.

(*Convivio* III.xiv.2–3 and 6)

This, then – philosophy as the love of wisdom pre-eminently in the divine mind and indeed constitutive of the divine mind – is Dante's new love, love, properly understood and carefully cultivated, thus making once again, as it always does in Dante, for an affirmation of self in the ever more ample substance of self, in the kind of transhumanity proper to humanity as but the most immanent of its immanent possibilities.

With what amounts, then, to an account of philosophy as an assimilation of the created to the uncreated mind and to this as the way of its proper happiness, we come to the first course proper of the banquet, where straightaway, however, we witness a foreshortening of perspective, a preoccupation less with philosophy in the round than with an issue in the area of moral philosophy in particular – with what, given the precise nature of Dante's readership in the *Convivio* (the "many men and women in this language of ours burdened by domestic and civic care"), it means to speak of 'gentilezza' or nobility as a property of historical selfhood. True, there are other considerations here, not least among them, Dante says, the difficulty he is having with philosophy in its more arcane reaches, in relation, more exactly, to the status of pure matter as an object of divine intentionality, all of which, he says, has had the effect of concentrating his mind upon lesser fare; but this, in truth, is a matter not so much of difficulty as of discovery, of his settling at last upon his true genius as a moral rather than a natural philosopher, as one engaged, that is to say, at the level less of the idea pure and simple than of its espousal as a means of positive being and becoming *ex parte subiecti*, on the part of the morally and ontologically anxious I-self. First, then, as far as 'gentilezza' is concerned, comes the antithesis, the idea of nobility as a matter of "ancient wealth and custom" (the "antica ricchezza e belli costumi" of IV.iii.6), a notion endorsed in its time both by the emperor Frederick II of Hohenstaufen and, as if that were not enough, by Aristotle – all of which means that, as a dissenting spirit, Dante must tread carefully. And this indeed he does, taking care before all else to establish *vis-à-vis* both the one and the other the basis of his dissent, of his daring to disagree. As far, then, as the emperor is concerned it is a question of his having *qua* emperor no right to pronounce here, imperial writ running absolutely only in matters of pure positive law, of those laws, that is to say, having about them no intrinsically moral component:

> Queste cose simigliantemente, che de l'altre arti sono ragionate, vedere si possono ne l'arte imperiale; ché regole sono in quella che sono pure arti, sì come sono le leggi de' matrimonii, de li servi, de le milizie, de li successori in dignitade, e di queste in tutto siamo a lo Imperadore subietti, sanza dubbio e sospetto alcuno. Altre leggi sono che sono quasi seguitatrici di natura, sì come constituire l'uomo d'etade sofficiente a ministrare, e di queste non semo in tutto subietti ...

> What we have said relative to the other arts holds good too with respect to the art of imperial government, for there are here rules after the manner of pure arts, such as the laws governing matrimony, slavery, military service and the inheritance of titles, in all of which we are without any doubt at all subject to the emperor. But there are other laws following on, so to speak, from nature, such as deciding how old a man must be before assuming public office, and here we are not entirely subject to him ...

> (*Convivio* IV.ix.14–15)

while as far as the Philosopher is concerned it is a question not so much of his having endorsed the idea as of his simply having noted it as a routine but scarcely persuasive assumption on the part of the commonalty. Dante, then, is on safe ground, there being here no question of *lèse-majesté*, of offending the powers that be.

With this, then, he gets down to the main business of this fourth book of the *Convivio*, his first task being to demolish the notion of wealth in particular as a principle of nobility properly understood. And here he has no real difficulty, indeed no difficulty whatsoever, for one has only to dwell for a moment on the substance and psychology of wealth – meaning by this material wealth in the most immediate and elementary sense of the term – to be impressed by its fundamental *ig*nobility. For material wealth in the most immediate and elementary sense of the term knows no point of arrival and thus no proper perfection, its only effect being to engender endless craving and endless anxiety:

> Promettono le false traditrici sempre, in certo numero adunate, rendere lo raunatore pieno d'ogni appagamento; e con questa promissione conducono l'umana volontade in vizio d'avarizia. E per questo le chiama Boezio, in quello De Consolatione, pericolose, dicendo: "Ohmè! chi fu quel primo che li pesi de l'oro coperto, e le pietre che si voleano ascondere, preziosi pericoli, cavoe?" Promettono le false traditrici, se bene si guarda, di torre ogni sete e ogni mancanza, e apportare ogni saziamento e bastanza; e questo fanno nel principio a ciascuno uomo, questa promissione in certa quantità di loro accrescimento affermando; e poi che quivi sono adunate, in loco di saziamento e di refrigerio danno e recano sete di casso febricante intollerabile; e in loco di bastanza recano nuovo termine, cioè maggiore quantitade a desiderio, e, con questa, paura grande e sollicitudine sopra l'acquisto. Sì che veramente non quietano, ma più danno cura, la qual prima sanza loro non si avea.

To those gathering them in sufficient quantity, these perfidious traitors forever promise satisfaction, a promise, however, conducive simply to the sin of avarice. That is why Boethius, in his *Consolation*, speaks of them as dangerous, saying: "Alas! Who was the first to unearth that mass of gold and gems, those precious perils, that sought to remain hidden?" These same traitors, should one study them closely, promise to do away with all desire and deficiency and to ensure complete satisfaction and sufficiency. That is what they do initially, guaranteeing the fulfilment of their promise once a certain amount has been reached. But once that amount *has* been reached, instead of sufficiency and spiritual refreshment, all they do is to create in the heart and mind of the individual nothing but an unbearably fevered thirst. Instead of satisfaction, they simply set up a new goal, a desire for still more, and, along with this, endless anxiety in respect of what has already been acquired. Theirs, rather than satisfaction, is simply suffering, an order of anxiety never there in the first place.

(Convivio IV.xii.4–5)

The notion of proper perfection and, with it, proper satisfaction is worth pausing over for a moment, for Dante's, typically, is a sense of human experience as but a series of discrete ends or objectives each qualitatively unique and each open to its own proper accomplishment; so, for example, and making once again for the dismissal of wealth pure and simple as a principle of properly human well-being and thus of properly human happiness, these lines from IV.xiii, secure in their sense of the strictly speaking 'successional' or periodic character of man's coming about as man:

A la questione rispondendo, dico che propriamente crescere lo desiderio de la scienza dire non si può, avvegna che, come detto è, per alcuno modo si dilati. Ché quello che propriamente cresce, sempre è uno; lo desiderio de la scienza non è sempre uno, ma è molti, e finito l'uno, viene l'altro; sì che, propriamente parlando, non è crescere lo suo dilatare, ma successione di picciola cosa in grande cosa. Che se io desidero di sapere li principii de le cose naturali, incontanente che io so questi, è compiuto e terminato questo desiderio. E se poi io desidero di sapere che cosa e com'è ciascuno di questi principii, questo è un altro desiderio nuovo, né per l'avvenimento di questo non mi si toglie la perfezione a la quale mi condusse l'altro; e questo cotale dilatare non è cagione d'imperfezione, ma di perfezione maggiore. Quello veramente de la ricchezza è propriamente crescere, ché è sempre pur uno, sì che nulla successione quivi si vede, e per nullo termine e per nulla perfezione.

I maintain, then, by way of response that the desire for knowledge cannot strictly be said to increase, although, as already noted, it expands in a certain way. For, strictly, whatever merely increases is always one, but the desire for knowledge is not always one, but, rather, many; for where one desire ends, another begins, so that, strictly speaking, its growth is a matter, not of *increase*, but, rather, of *succession*, of a movement from the lesser to the greater. For if I wish to know the principles of natural things, as soon as I know them that wish is fulfilled and comes to an end. If I then seek to know the precise nature and modality of each one of these principles then that is a fresh and distinct desire. Nor by the advent of that new desire do I forfeit the satisfaction of my first desire, this development being a matter, not of imperfection, but of still greater perfection. In the case of riches, however, it is simply a matter of growth pure and simple, there being here, therefore, no discernible succession or end or perfection.

(*Convivio* IV.xiii.1–2)

– lines to which, as bearing again on the step-by-step or graduated character of human experience properly understood, of its unfolding, that is to say, by way not merely – indeed not at all – of more of the same, but of a progression from one peak of perfection to another on the planes of knowing and loving, we may note these lines from early on in the *Paradiso*:

"O amanza del primo amante, o diva",
diss' io appresso, "il cui parlar m'inonda
e scalda sì, che più e più m'avviva,
  non è l'affezion mia tanto profonda,
che basti a render voi grazia per grazia;
ma quei che vede e puote a ciò risponda.
  Io veggio ben che già mai non si sazia
nostro intelletto, se 'l ver non lo illustra
di fuor dal qual nessun vero si spazia.
  Posasi in esso, come fera in lustra,
tosto che giunto l'ha; e giugner puollo:
se non, ciascun disio sarebbe *frustra*.
  Nasce per quello, a guisa di rampollo,
a piè del vero il dubbio; ed è natura
ch'al sommo pinge noi di collo in collo".

"O beloved of the first lover, o divine one," said I then, "whose speech so floods and warms me such that I am ever more quickened, my affection for all its depth is scarce sufficient to render you grace for grace; but may he who sees and can indeed do so answer thereunto. Well do I see that never can our intellect be wholly satisfied unless there shine on it that truth beyond which no truth extends. Therein it rests, as a wild beast in his lair, so soon as it has reached it; and reach it it can, else every desire would be in vain. Our questioning thus springs up like a shoot at the foot of the truth, nature itself thus peak by peak urging us on to the summit."

(*Paradiso* IV.118–32)

And what applies to wealth as the ground of nobility applies also to ancestry, for ancestry pure and simple, to the exclusion, that is to say, of all else, leaves no room for emergence, for the possibility of a base-born son making good by way of the properties of personality:

Dove è da sapere che oppinione di questi erranti è che uomo prima villano mai gentile uomo dicer non si possa; né uomo che figlio sia di villano similemente dicere mai non si possa gentile. E ciò rompe la loro sentenza medesima, quando dicono che tempo si richiede a nobilitade, ponendo questo vocabulo "antico"; però ch'è impossibile per processo di tempo venire a la generazione di nobilitade per questa loro ragione che detta è, la quale toglie via che villano uomo mai possa esser gentile per opera che faccia, o per alcuno accidente, e toglie via la mutazione di villano padre in gentile figlio. Che se lo figlio del villano è pur villano, e lo figlio fia pur figlio di villano e così fia anche villano, e anche suo figlio, e così sempre, e mai non s'avrà a trovare là dove nobilitade per processo di tempo si cominci.

The view, then, of those misguided souls – and this is what we need to understand here – is that neither a man of lowly stock nor one born of a man of lowly stock can ever be deemed noble. But it is at this point that, speaking thus of time as a prerequisite of nobility (the term they use here being "ancestral") their argument collapses, for it is not possible in the order of time alone to speak of the coming about of nobility, their own reasoning ruling out the possibility either of a man basely born ever by dint of his own activity or by chance becoming noble or of the son of such a man enjoying a like change in status. For if the son of a man basely born is himself basely born, then so also is the son of a son of a man thus basely born, and his son too, and so on forever, there being no point in the order of time at which nobility actually begins.

(*Convivio* IV.xiv.3–4)

All in all, then, neither wealth nor lineage will do as a way of seeing and understanding nobility in its new social and civic context, at which point, therefore, Dante turns his attention less to what it is not than to what it is, namely – and on analogy with the sky as the *locus* or whereabouts of the stars – the encompassing of every refinement both spiritual and physical in man, of every comeliness both of the mind and of the body. The key passage here, notable again only for its rejoicing, for its sense of man as – in respect, precisely, of his multiple perfection and perfectibility – created not a little lower but a little higher than the angels, reads as follows:

Dice dunque: *Sì comè 'l cielo dovunquè la stella*, e non è questo vero *e converso*, cioè rivolto, che dovunque è cielo sia la stella, così è nobilitade dovunque è vertude, e non vertude dovunque nobilitade; e con bello e convenevole essemplo, ché veramente è cielo ne lo quale molte e diverse stelle rilucono. Riluce in essa le intellettuali e le morali virtudi; riluce in essa le buone disposizioni da natura date, cioè pietade e religione, e le laudabili passioni, cioè vergogna e misericordia e altre molte; riluce in essa le corporali bontadi, cioè bellezza, fortezza e quasi perpetua valitudine. E tante sono le sue stelle, che del cielo risplendono, che certo non è da maravigliare se molti e diversi frutti fanno ne la umana nobilitade; tante sono le nature e le potenze di quella, in una sotto una semplice sustanza comprese e adunate, ne le quali sì come in diversi rami fruttifica diversamente. Certo da dovvero ardisco a dire che la nobilitade umana, quanto è da la parte di molti suoi frutti, quella de l'angelo soperchia, tuttoché l'angelica in sua unitade sia più divina.

Next, then, the text says: *As wherever there is a star there is sky –* though not always the other way round such that wherever there is sky there is a star, for although there is always nobility where there is virtue, there is not always virtue where there is nobility. The analogy is as beautiful as it is fitting, for nobility is truly a heaven in which any number of different stars shine. In it shine the intellectual and moral virtues, just as in it shine those worthy dispositions of the soul bestowed by nature, namely piety, religion and such praiseworthy feelings as modesty, mercy and much else besides, not to mention beauty, strength and good health as pertaining in their excellence to the flesh. So numerous are the stars scattered throughout the heavens that it is no wonder that human nature in its nobility bears in consequence so many and so diverse fruits, fruits endlessly varied in both kind and potentiality and all of them gathered into and comprehended by a single substance, whence, as though on different branches, they come to maturity. Indeed, I would go so far as to say that, though theirs, in the simplicity of their being, is more divine, human nobility, in its manifold fruitfulness, is greater than that of the angels themselves.

(*Convivio* IV.xix. 5–6)

But descending for a moment from the rapturous to the reasonable, it is possible to be more exact as to the nature and genesis of nobility thus understood, for nobility thus understood, Dante explains, is but the "seed of happiness implanted by God in the well-disposed soul", a proposition open to development in terms of how that seed stands to be sown both in good and in poor soil, both in the deserving and in the undeserving alike. Taking first, then, the general proposition, and noting as we do so its at once Pauline and Guinizzellian authorization (Paul to the effect that all good gifts come from above and Guinizzelli to the effect that only the purest of gem stones is capable of receiving and reflecting such power as emanates from the heavens), we may say this, that nobility, properly understood, is a question of divine insemination, of God's gracing those already disposed by nature to host the seed of properly human happiness sown from on high:

Ultimamente conchiude, e dice che, per quello che dinanzi detto è (cioè che le vertudi sono frutto di nobilitade, e che Dio questa metta ne l'anima che ben siede), che *ad alquanti*, cioè a quelli che hanno intelletto, che sono pochi, è manifesto che nobilitade umana non sia altro che "seme di felicitade", *messo da Dio ne l'anima ben posta*, cioè lo cui corpo è d'ogni parte disposto perfettamente ... E così è diffinita questa nostra bontade, la quale in noi similemente discende da somma e spirituale virtude, come virtude in pietra da corpo nobilissimo celestiale.

And so finally, and on the basis of everything said so far relative to virtue as but the fruit of nobility and to this as implanted by God in the soul well settled in the body, the text concludes by saying that *to those few* – to those, that is to say, of lively intelligence (few indeed) – man's proper nobility is nothing other than the 'seed of happiness' *infused by God in the well-disposed soul*, that is, in the soul whose body is in every respect perfectly ready to receive it ... This, then, is how we are to understand our proper goodness, the goodness that, after the manner of a precious stone that receives its power from the noblest of the heavenly bodies, comes to us from the supreme spiritual power on high.

(Convivio IV.xx.9–10)

By way, therefore, of explaining how this seed of happiness is sown from on high, Dante offers a little embryology, an account of how, at the point of conception, the sensitive soul generated *ex materia* is at last taken up in the rational soul as a matter of divine inspiration or in-breathing. The male seed, then, entering the matrix of the womb and addressing the embryo, so disposes it as to receive the power of the heavens by which it is quickened, whereupon, in yet a fresh moment of divine creativity, the possible intellect as that part of the rational soul open to the reception of pure form is breathed into it from beyond – the whole thing making for something not now just a little lower than the angels but for just about another God incarnate:

E però dico che quando l'umano seme cade nel suo recettaculo, cioè ne la matrice, esso porta seco la vertù de l'anima generativa e la vertù del cielo e la vertù de li elementi legati, cioè la complessione; e matura e dispone la materia a la vertù formativa, la quale diede l'anima del generante; e la vertù formativa prepara li organi a la vertù celestiale, che produce de la potenza del seme l'anima in vita. La quale, incontanente produtta, riceve da la vertù del motore del cielo lo intelletto possibile; lo quale potenzialmente in sé adduce tutte le forme universali, secondo che sono nel suo produttore, e tanto meno quanto più dilungato da la prima Intelligenza è ... E sono alcuni di tale oppinione che dicono, se tutte le precedenti vertudi s'accordassero sovra la produzione d'un'anima ne la loro ottima disposizione, che tanto discenderebbe in quella de la deitade, che quasi sarebbe un altro Iddio incarnato.

I say, then, that when the human seed enters the womb, it bears with it the power of the generative soul, the power of heaven, and the power of the elements in their precise complexion or combination one with another. There, it matures and disposes matter to receive the formative power brought by the soul of the male parent, and this formative power readies the organs to receive the celestial power that actualizes the latent power of the seed to life. As soon as this is brought into being, it receives from the almighty mover of the heavens the possible intellect as in potential to every kind of universal form as present to the One who brings it into being, though, in proportion to its distance from the primal intelligence, in a greater or lesser degree ... There are even some who claim that if all the preceding powers were to be optimally conjoined one with another in the moment of bringing forth a soul, then such would be the divine substance of that soul that it would be well-nigh another God incarnate.

(*Convivio* IV.xxi.4–5 and 10)

But there is more, for in circumstances of a seed duly sown but either deficient or poorly cultivated, or even of there being no seed at all to speak of, there is always room for the grafting on of good upon faulty stock or even of fresh insemination, all of which rules out there ever being any excuse in human experience for ignobility; for one way or another all men are in a position to lay hold of their proper happiness and thus of their proper humanity as creatures of reasonable moral determination:

E in questo ... è nostra beatitudine e somma felicitade, sì
come vedere si può; la quale è la dolcezza del sopra notato
seme, sì come omai manifestamente appare, a la quale molte
volte cotale seme non perviene per male essere coltivato, e per
essere disviata la sua pullulazione. E similemente puote essere,
per molta correzione e cultura, che là dove questo seme dal
principio non cade, si puote inducere [n]el suo processo, sì
che perviene a questo frutto; ed è uno modo quasi d'insetare
l'altrui natura sopra diversa radice. E però nullo è che possa
essere scusato; ché se da sua naturale radice uomo non ha
questa sementa, ben la puote avere per via d'insetazione. Così
fossero tanti quelli di fatto che s'insetassero, quanti sono quelli
che da la buona radice si lasciano disviare!

Herein, then ... in the sweetness of the aforesaid seed, lie as is
plain to see our every blessing and joy. Often enough, it is true,
that seed does not by reason of poor cultivation or disorderly
growth come to proper fruition. But this may likewise be
attained by careful cultivation, for even where the seed was
not there from the outset it can be encouraged to grow and
to bear fruit by way of the kind of grafting whereby a plant
is raised from other rootstock. There can, then, be no excuse
for anyone, for if a man lacks this seed by nature, it can even
so be his by way of insemination. Indeed would to God there
were as many made good by insemination as there are astray
in respect of the good stock properly theirs!

(*Convivio* IV.xxii.11–12)

With what amounts, then, to – socially and politically speaking –
an at once more properly persuasive and more properly responsible
account of nobility in terms of its status (*a*) as the encompassing in
respect of every moral and intellectual excellence in man, and (*b*) as
the proper patrimony of all men, it only remains to describe its manifestation or showing forth over the arc of life as a whole, over the
four ages of man in his adolescence, his early manhood, his seniority and his senescence. First, then, and extending to his twenty-fifth

year, comes his "adolescenza", where it is a question of the decorum, deference and discretion making for a modest and properly proportionate presence in the world, for the acknowledgement of one's elders and betters, for a certain shyness and self-possession, and for proper care in respect of one's outward aspect ("for due order among the bodily members makes for a sense of harmony at once delightful to behold and beyond words to describe"). Then, with his emergence into young manhood (lasting now from his twenty-fifth to his forty-fifth year), comes the strength of spirit whereby he presides in an orderly way over his own humanity, the solicitude whereby he looks to the well-being both of his juniors and of his seniors, the courtesy whereby he engages civilly with his neighbours, and the loyalty whereby he honours the constitution and, as by nature a righteous spirit, takes pleasure in so doing. Next, and more than ordinarily gracious in point both of conception and of expression, comes seniority as extending from a man's forty-fifth to his seventieth year, this being the moment in which, like a rose in its maturity, personality opens up in all its now seasoned substance to spread abroad its sweet fragrance, the fragrance of its now accumulated wisdom:

Dunque appresso la propria perfezione, la quale s'acquista ne la gioventute, conviene venire quella che alluma non pur sé ma li altri; e conviensi aprire l'uomo quasi com'una rosa che più chiusa stare non puote, e l'odore che dentro generato è spandere.

Following on, then, from the perfection of self as the accomplishment of maturity, it is proper now that that perfection illumine not simply self but others too. It is proper that, like a rose content no longer to stay closed, a man too opens up, spreading abroad as he does so the fragrance generated within.

(*Convivio* IV.xxvii.4)

This, then, is but the sweet fragrance of discretion, of wise and generous counsel, of justice in framing and administering the law, of kindliness in dealing with others, and of eloquence and affability. And then, finally, there is senescence or advanced age, where, having lived out and rejoiced in the virtues of adolescence, maturity and seniority, the virtues, that is to say, of deference, decisiveness and generous counsel respectively, a man looks back, blesses the course of his existence so far, and prepares now to lower the sails of his barque with a view to slipping gently into port, this, then, being the moment of anticipation, the moment in which the attentive spirit sets aside every mortal preoccupation in favour of the qualitatively other of what now is to come:

Appresso de la ragionata particola è da procedere a l'ultima, cioè a quella che comincia: *Poi ne la quarta parte de la vita*; per la quale lo testo intende mostrare quello che fa la nobile anima ne l'ultima etade, cioè nel senio. E dice ch'ella fa due cose: l'una, che ella ritorna a Dio, sì come a quello porto onde ella si partio quando venne ad intrare nel mare di questa vita; l'altra si è, che ella benedice lo cammino che ha fatto, però che è stato diritto e buono, e sanza amaritudine di tempesta. E qui è da sapere, che, sì come dice Tullio in quello De Senectute, la naturale morte è quasi a noi porto di lunga navigazione e riposo. Ed è così: [ché], come lo buono marinaio, come esso appropinqua al porto, cala le sue vele, e soavemente, con debile conducimento, entra in quello; così noi dovemo calare le vele de le nostre mondane operazioni e tornare a Dio con tutto nostro intendimento e cuore, sì che a quello porto si vegna con tutta soavitade e con tutta pace.

Having got this far in our account of the text we must turn now to its last part, the part beginning *And then in the final phase of a man's life*, where its aim is to show how nobility expresses itself towards the end, in extreme old age. The soul, it says, does two things: it turns to God as to the port whence it departed when it first set out on the ocean of this life, and it blesses the journey now completed, a journey direct, wholesome and untroubled by storm and tempest. Indeed, it is good to remember here that, as Tully says in his book *On Old Age*, natural death is, as it were, a port or haven at the end of a long voyage, a place of rest. And that indeed is how it is, for just as a good sailor, on approaching a port, lowers his sails and slips more than ever gently into it, so ought we to lower the sails of our worldly affairs and turn to God with all our heart and mind, thus coming home with all sweetness and peace.

(*Convivio* IV.xxviii.1–3)

Here especially, then, commitment, accountability, responsibility and the busyness generally of the active life give way to a gentle interiority, to a quiet anticipation of homecoming and of the welcome afforded by those rejoicing already in the immediate presence of God (the exquisite and already perfectly paradisal "a la nobile anima si fanno incontro, e deono fare, quelli cittadini de la etterna vita" of IV.xxviii.5).

With this, then, Dante's meditation on the substance and phenomenology of nobility in its civic aspect is complete, but for all its nothing if not exalted sense of 'gentilezza' as the seed of happiness implanted by God in the well-disposed soul, and for all its celebration of the four ages of man in terms of their discretion, their courage, their generosity and their gentle anticipation of the blessedness to come, his withal is a meditation informed from out of the depths by a blend of anger and sadness, now the one now the other moving centre-stage. On the one hand, then, the anger engendered by those merely playing at nobility, and playing at it, moreover, at the expense of the widow and the orphan:

Ahi malestrui e malnati, che disertate vedove e pupilli, che rapite a li men possenti, che furate e occupate l'altrui ragioni; e di quelle corredate conviti, donate cavalli e arme, robe e denari, portate le mirabili vestimenta, edificate li mirabili edifici, e credetevi larghezza fare! E che è questo altro a fare che levare lo drappo di su l'altare e coprire lo ladro la sua mensa? … Udite, ostinati, che dice Tullio contro a voi nel libro de li Offici: "Sono molti, certo desiderosi d'essere apparenti e gloriosi, che tolgono a li altri per dare a li altri, credendosi buoni essere tenuti, [se li] arricchiscono per qual ragione essere voglia. Ma ciò tanto è contrario a quello che far si conviene, che nulla è più".

Alas, you ill-starred and ill-begotten, you who despoil widows and orphans, who plunder the most helpless, who steal and appropriate what belongs to others, with all of which you put on banquets, you bestow one upon another horses and weapons, goods and money, you sport splendid gowns and build magnificent palaces, all in the name of munificence. How does this differ from a thief's making off with the cloth from the altar and covering his table with it? ... Pay heed, you of obstinate spirit, to the harsh words Cicero has for you in his *On Offices*: "There are many people who, in their eagerness to cut a fine figure and gain renown, take from one to give to another, thinking they will be honoured no matter how they obtain the largesse they distribute; but there is nothing, but nothing, more completely opposed to what they should be doing."

(*Convivio* IV.xxvii.13–15)

while on the other hand, the sadness everywhere engendered by the spectacle of a civilization lost to its civility, style – meaning by this the *anaphora* and the *exclamatio* of a superbly constructed period – thus stepping in to confirm the twofold substance and intensity of Dante's discourse in the *Convivio*, a discourse turning, precisely, upon the social and civic *angst* of it all:

Oh misera, misera patria mia! quanta pietà mi stringe per te, qual volta leggo, qual volta scrivo cosa che a reggimento civile abbia rispetto!

O wretched, wretched country of mine! How overwhelmed I am with pity for you whenever I read or whenever I write aught to do with civil government!

(*Convivio* IV.xxvii.11)

PROBLEMS OF PERSPECTIVE AND A CIVIC ONTOLOGY

What, then, are we to say about the *Convivio* – about the nothing if not magnanimous or 'large-souled' *Convivio* – in the round? Something along these lines: that, for all its magnanimity – its fervent commitment, that is to say, to the well-being of the next man – the *Convivio* is at its most eloquent when it comes to the as yet unresolved structure of Dante's own being, this in turn, and indeed in the very moment of its conception, making for its inevitable incompletion, for its foundering upon a tension operative from out of the depths.

Taking first, then, this latter aspect of the text, we may say this, that, if on the one hand the *Convivio* bears witness in something approaching its pure form to Dante's faith in philosophy precisely as such – as but the love of wisdom – as the way of man's properly human happiness, then his even so, and indeed in one and the same moment, is a characteristic toing and froing between the immanent and the transcendent poles of his inspiration, between the kind of happiness proper to man in consequence of his status as a creature of free moral and intellectual determination and the kind accruing to him by way of a gracious assimilation of self to the other and greater than self. True, both at the beginning and at the end of his career as a poet and philosopher, both in the *Vita nova* and in the *Commedia* as the expression of his respectively youthful and seasoned spirituality, there is a coalescence of these things within the economy of the whole, grace and its power to transfiguration entering into nature and its power to significant self-determination as but its quickening, as that whereby it is confirmed and perfected in its proper operation. But here in the *Convivio* they subsist to the point of threatening the unity, the consistency and, again, the completability of the text. On the one hand, then, we have the ecstatic moment represented by Books II and III, 'ecstatic' in the sense of – the busy lives of his chosen readership notwithstanding – Dante's launching upon an account of philosophy as but a participation in the life and light of the Godhead, as that whereby those enamoured of wisdom are fashioned afresh in the likeness of their maker; so, for example – and more than ever rapt in point both of conception and of expression – these lines on the sweet 'demonstrations' and 'persuasions' of Wisdom (her eyes and her smile respectively) as but the vesture and outshining of her inner and abiding light, and, as far as the beholder is concerned, of these things as but the principle of his or her proper perfection:

Dice adunque lo testo "che ne la faccia di costei appariscono cose che mostrano de' piaceri di Paradiso"; e distingue lo loco dove ciò appare, cioè ne li occhi e ne lo riso. E qui si conviene sapere che li occhi de la Sapienza sono le sue demonstrazioni, con le quali si vede la veritade certissimamente; e lo suo riso sono le sue persuasioni, ne le quali si dimostra la luce interiore de la Sapienza sotto alcuno velamento: e in queste due cose si sente quel piacere altissimo di beatitudine, lo quale è massimo bene in Paradiso. Questo piacere in altra cosa di qua giù essere non può, se non nel guardare in questi occhi e in questo riso. E la ragione è questa: che, con ciò sia cosa che ciascuna cosa naturalmente disia la sua perfezione, sanza quella essere non può [l'uomo] contento, che è essere beato; ché quantunque l'altre cose avesse, sanza questa rimarrebbe in lui desiderio: lo quale essere non può con la beatitudine, acciò che la beatitudine sia perfetta cosa e lo desiderio sia cosa defettiva; ché nullo desidera quello che ha, ma quello che non ha, che è manifesto difetto. E in questo sguardo solamente l'umana perfezione s'acquista, cioè la perfezione de la ragione, de la quale, sì come di principalissima parte, tutta la nostra essenza depende; e tutte l'altre nostre operazioni sentire, nutrire, e tutto sono per quella sola, e questa è per sé, e non per altri; sì che, perfetta sia questa, perfetta è quella, tanto cioè che l'uomo, in quanto ello è uomo, vede terminato ogni desiderio, e così è beato.

The text says then "that in her face there appear things that manifest some part of the joy of Paradise", and it identifies the place where it appears, namely her eyes and her smile. What then we need to understand here is that the eyes of wisdom are her demonstrations, by which truth is seen with the greatest certainty, and her smiles are her persuasions, in which the inner light of wisdom is revealed behind a kind of veil; and in each of them is felt the highest joy of blessedness, which is the greatest good of paradise. This joy cannot be found in anything here below except by looking into her eyes and upon her smile. The reason for this is that since everything by nature desires its own perfection, without this perfection man could not be happy, that is to say, could not be blessed; for even if he had every other thing, by lacking this perfection desire would still be present in him, and desire is something that cannot coexist with blessedness since blessedness is something perfect and desire something defective; for no one desires what he has but rather what he does not have, which is an obvious deficiency. It is in this gaze alone that human perfection is acquired (that is, the perfection of reason), on which, since it is our foremost part, all our being depends; and all of our other activities (feeling, nutrition and the rest) exist only for the sake of this, and this exists for its own sake and not for the sake of anything else. Therefore if this is perfect, so is the other, to the extent that man, insofar as he is man, sees all his desires brought to their end and is thereby blessed.

(*Convivio* III.xv.2–4)

On the other hand, and ranged over against the *transcendent* moment of the text, its preoccupation, that is to say, with philosophy and the pursuit thereof as but a matter of assimilation, of a forever fresh making over of the creature in the likeness of the creator, we have its *immanent* moment, a proportioning of the philosophical enterprise to what man already is and to what he can already say and do as a creature of moral and intellectual determination. There are two passages to consider here, the first of which, on the threshold of Book IV, registers in the way we have seen Dante's settling at last upon his true genius as a philosopher – as, more precisely, a *moral* as distinct from a *natural* philosopher. Having, he says, suffered the indifference of My Lady Philosophy when it came to a nothing if not esoteric issue in the area of divine intentionality, he turned instead to the more manageable notion of 'gentilezza' or properly human nobility, 'more manageable' in its turning upon the *what* and *how* of human understanding in its more practical aspect:

> Per che, con ciò fosse cosa che questa mia donna un poco li suoi dolci sembianti transmutasse a me, massimamente in quelle parti dove io mirava e cercava se la prima materia de li elementi era da Dio intesa, – per la qual cosa un poco dal frequentare lo suo aspetto mi sostenni –, quasi ne la sua assenzia dimorando, entrai a riguardare col pensiero lo difetto umano intorno al detto errore. E per fuggire oziositade, che massimamente di questa donna è nemica, e per istinguere questo errore che tanti amici le toglie, proposi di gridare a la gente che per mal cammino andavano, acciò che per diritto calle si dirizzassero; e cominciai una canzone nel cui principio dissi: *Le dolci rime d'amor ch'i' solia*. Ne la quale io intendo riducer la gente in diritta via sopra la propia conoscenza de la verace nobilitade; sì come per la conoscenza del suo testo, a la esposizione del quale ora s'intende, vedere si potrà.

Now it happened that my lady ceased to reveal herself to me with quite her accustomed sweetness, particularly as regards my seeking to know whether the prime matter of the elements was an object of divine knowledge. Consequently, I refrained for a time from attempting to see her, and, since I now passed my time without her company, I gave my attention to the error of men on the above subject. Wishing, therefore, to avoid idleness as the chief enemy of this lady, and to do away once and for all with an error depriving her of so many friends, I settled on proclaiming the truth hereabouts to those astray in order that they might direct their steps aright. I thus set about composing a canzone which begins *The sweet rhymes I once used* and in which – as will be evident from a reading of the text on which I'm about to comment – it is my intention to get

people back on track when it comes to a proper understanding
of nobility in its essential nature.

(*Convivio* IV.i.8–9)

– while clearing the way for everything coming next in this fourth
book of the *Convivio*, we have this passage from the final chapter
of the third book, scarcely less than peremptory in its dismissal of
the caviller concerned in respect of the usefulness of it all – of the
value of philosophy, that is to say, as the love of wisdom coeval and
consubstantial with the Godhead – to the man in the street, to the
"many men and women in this language of ours burdened by civic
and domestic care". Let the caviller therefore hold his peace, for
in truth we *wish* to know here and now only what we *can* know
here and now, anything else, Dante insists, being an overshooting
of the mark – at which point his foreshortening of the intellectual
perspective is as sudden as it is stark:

Veramente può qui alcuno forte dubitare come ciò sia,
che la sapienza possa fare l'uomo beato, non potendo a lui
perfettamente certe cose mostrare; con ciò sia cosa che 'l naturale
desiderio sia a l'uomo di sapere, e sanza compiere lo desiderio
beato essere non possa. A ciò si può chiaramente rispondere
che lo desiderio naturale in ciascuna cosa è misurato secondo
la possibilitade de la cosa desiderante; altrimenti andrebbe
in contrario di sé medesimo, che impossibile è; e la Natura
l'avrebbe fatto indarno, che è anche impossibile. In contrario
andrebbe, ché, desiderando la sua perfezione, desiderrebbe la sua
imperfezione; imperò che desiderrebbe sé sempre desiderare e
non compiere mai suo desiderio (e in questo errore cade l'avaro
maladetto, e non s'accorge che desidera sé sempre desiderare,
andando dietro al numero impossibile a giungere). Avrebbelo
anco la Natura fatto indarno, però che non sarebbe ad alcuno
fine ordinato. E però l'umano desiderio è misurato in questa
vita a quella scienza che qui avere si può, e quello punto non
passa se non per errore, lo quale è di fuori di naturale intenzione.

E così è misurato ne la natura angelica, e terminato, in quanto, in quella sapienza che la natura di ciascuno può apprendere. E questa è la ragione per che li Santi non hanno tra loro invidia, però che ciascuno aggiugne lo fine del suo desiderio, lo quale desiderio è con la bontà de la natura misurato. Onde, con ciò sia cosa che conoscere di Dio e di certe altre cose quello esse sono non sia possibile a la nostra natura, quello da noi naturalmente non è desiderato di sapere. E per questo è la dubitazione soluta.

There may in truth be some, however, who doubt whether wisdom can make a man happy if by it certain things cannot be made known to him, for man has a natural desire to know, which, unless satisfied, cannot make him happy. To this we may reply quite simply that natural desire in anything whatever is proportionate to the possibility of its fulfilment, for otherwise it would be forever going against its own nature, something not only impossible in itself, but which – no less impossibly – would entail nature's having made it in vain. It would be going against itself in that, while desiring perfection, it would in fact be desiring *im*perfection, since it would go on desiring and desiring without ever satisfying that desire (this being the mistake of the miser who, in his perversity, fails to understand that in seeking out an infinitely open-ended goal he desires only to desire). And nature would have created it in vain in that it would be directed to no specific end. Therefore human desire in this life is proportionate to the wisdom to be had here, and never is the limit overshot other than by way of something foreign to nature's intention. So it is with the angels, their desire being limited only by what they can see and understand. That too is why the saints are free from envy one of another, for each, in desiring in a manner consonant with their proper goodness, has reached the limit of his desiring. And that is why, since it is not within the reach of our nature to know either God in his essence or any number of similar things besides, we do not naturally desire to know these things. Thus the issue is resolved.

(*Convivio* III.xv.7–10)

– lines to which, as all of a piece with this in point of the now revised perspective of the text, we may add these from Book IV with their unqualified sense of Aristotle not merely as the finisher of all moral philosophy but as guide *par excellence* to properly human happiness. Have a good read of Aristotle, Dante insists, and you cannot but be a happy man:

> Veramente Aristotile, che Stagirite ebbe sopranome, e Zenocrate Calcedonio, suo compagnone, [per lo studio loro], e per lo 'ngegno [eccellente] e quasi divino che la natura in Aristotile messo avea, questo fine conoscendo per lo modo socratico quasi e academico, limaro e a perfezione la filosofia morale redussero, e massimamente Aristotile. E però che Aristotile cominciò a disputare andando in qua e in lae, chiamati furono – lui, dico, e li suoi compagni – Peripatetici, che tanto vale quanto 'deambulatori'. E però che la perfezione di questa moralitade per Aristotile terminata fue, lo nome de li Academici si spense, e tutti quelli che a questa setta si presero Peripatetici sono chiamati; e tiene questa gente oggi lo reggimento del mondo in dottrina per tutte parti, e puotesi appellare quasi cattolica oppinione. Per che vedere si può, Aristotile essere additatore e conduttore de la gente a questo segno.

In truth, then, Aristotle, surnamed the Stagirite, and his companion Xenocrates of Chalcedon (but especially Aristotle), by way of their study and of the singular – one might almost say divine – intelligence bestowed by nature upon the former, exploring this goal by much the same methods as Socrates and the Academics, refined and perfected the science of moral philosophy. Since, then, moral philosophy was perfected by Aristotle, the name Academic faded from memory, everyone associated with his circle being called Peripatetics (so called because Aristotle began his deliberations walking up and down, this being the meaning of the word). Today, the teaching of this group holds sway everywhere, theirs, we might say, being the orthodox view. Clearly, then, Aristotle is the one who directs and guides mankind to the goal we have been discussing.

(*Convivio* IV.vi.15–16)

This, then, is what it means to speak of the eloquence of the *Convivio* under its confessional aspect, as testimony, that is to say, to a crisis not merely of cultural allegiance but of temperament itself as calling from out of the depths for further resolution, for a fresh integration one with another of its most cherished concerns. But – and this for the moment is what matters – crises on the surface of the text and in the depths, decisive as they are for an overall interpretation of the *Convivio* and for any account of the place it occupies within Dante's spiritual itinerary as a whole, impact not in the least upon the solicitousness of the text as an essay in properly human being and becoming, in the laying hold by this or that individual or group of individuals of the deep reasons of his, her or their properly human presence in the world in all the distinctiveness, dignity and rapt substance thereof. For the *Convivio*, like everything else in Dante, is from first to last a text committed to the human project precisely as such, to the emergence of self into the fullness of its proper humanity as but the final cause and point of arrival of its each successive emphasis. Throughout then – from Book I with its account of the psychology of giving and receiving all the way through to its review in Book IV of nobility as variously pertaining to the individual in his or her adolescence, maturity, seniority and senescence – the pattern is the same, the text at every stage rejoicing in the humanity that it commends as the first and final cause of the soul's every sincere desire. In this sense at least, then – though this, to be sure, is an 'at least' of huge proportions – the *Convivio*, less than fully settled as it is, flows majestically into the *mare magnum* of the *Commedia* as but a reply to its each and every anxiety.

FOUR

The *Commedia*

PRELIMINARY CONSIDERATIONS: SPIRITUAL JOURNEYING
and the courage to be – a song of ascents: the *Commedia à la
lettre* – journeying under the aspect of seeing (*Inferno*) – journeying
under the aspect of striving (*Purgatorio*) – journeying under the aspect
of surpassing (*Paradiso*).

PRELIMINARY CONSIDERATIONS: SPIRITUAL
JOURNEYING AND THE COURAGE TO BE

The *Commedia* – the monumental *Commedia* – is the great work of
Dante's maturity, its greatness being manifold. If, then, notionally it
is a question of bringing home the philosophical to the theological
such that the latter constitutes the deep substance and indeed the
encompassing of the former, expressively it is a question of the
equality of the still youthful *lingua di sì* to every inflexion of
the spirit from the most sordid to the most sublime and of the
primordiality of the image as the means of spiritual intelligence,
as that whereby we enter into the "deepest places of human self-
destruction and despair as well as the highest places of courage
and salvation". And anxious as we are to settle upon what actually
and ultimately matters about Dante, and more precisely upon what
it is about the *Commedia* that speaks still to our condition, it is
upon the 'courage' element of Tillich's splendid formula that we
must settle as the point-about-which of our meditation. For if at
the literal level it is a question of the "state of souls after death" (the
"status animarum post mortem" of the letter to Cangrande della

Scala), it is at the same time, and by way now of an *immanent* as distinct from an *ultimate* eschatology, a question of the *what will be* of human experience under the aspect of eternity as but a definitive statement of the *what already is* of that experience as verifiable in the depths of the historical instant. And if again at the literal level it is a question of the state of souls after death, of the hell, purgatory and paradise to come, it is at the same time, and by virtue now of its first-person conception and articulation, an essay in spiritual journeying here and now, in what by way of the most complete kind of *self-confrontation*, *self-reconfiguration* and *self-transcendence* it means to be under way as a pilgrim spirit this side of the bar. In neither sense, therefore, can there be any looking the other way or passing by on the other side where the *Commedia* is concerned, for in both these respects it is a question of the at once suffering, striving and smiling substance of this or that instance of specifically human being under the conditions of time and space – of, in short, a Dasein analytic of terrifying power and precision.

A SONG OF ASCENTS: THE *COMMEDIA À LA LETTRE*

But with this we are getting ahead of ourselves, for here as with the *Vita nova* and the *Convivio* we need to consider the course of the argument as preliminary in respect of what actually and ultimately matters about it. Straightaway, then, and in a manner privileging from the outset the image as the means of moral, psychological and ontological elucidation, comes an account of the pilgrim poet – of Dante himself as protagonist in his own poem – as ranged over against self in the forum of conscience, as seeing the best but clinging to the worst:

> Nel mezzo del cammin di nostra vita
> mi ritrovai per una selva oscura,
> ché la diritta via era smarrita.
> Ahi quanto a dir qual era è cosa dura
> esta selva selvaggia e aspra e forte
> che nel pensier rinova la paura!

Tant'è amara che poco è più morte;
ma per trattar del ben ch'i' vi trovai,
dirò de l'altre cose ch'i' v'ho scorte.
  Io non so ben ridir com'i' v'intrai,
tant'era pien di sonno a quel punto
che la verace via abbandonai.
  Ma poi ch'i' fui al piè d'un colle giunto,
là dove terminava quella valle
che m'avea di paura il cor compunto,
  guardai in alto, e vidi le sue spalle
vestite già de' raggi del pianeta
che mena dritto altrui per ogne calle.
  Allor fu la paura un poco queta,
che nel lago del cor m'era durata
la notte ch'i' passai con tanta pieta

   ...

  Ed una lupa, che di tutte brame
sembiava carca ne la sua magrezza,
e molte genti fé già viver grame,
  questa mi porse tanto di gravezza
con la paura ch'uscia di sua vista,
ch'io perdei la speranza de l'altezza.

Midway in the journey of our life I found myself in a dark
wood, for the straight way was lost. Try as I may, there is no
telling how it was with that wood, so wild, rugged and harsh
was it that even to think of it terrifies me afresh! So savage, in
fact, that death itself is scarcely more. But for the sake of the
good I found there, I'll tell of what else I saw. How I came to
be there I cannot rightly say, so drowsy was I in the moment
I forsook the true way, but when I had reached the foot of a
hill at the far end of that valley, a valley that had so pierced
my heart with fear, I looked up and saw its shoulders swathed
already with the beams of that planet leading men aright on
every path. Then was assuaged a little the fear that, for the
night I had spent so grievously, had persisted in the lake of

my heart ... and a she-wolf that in her leanness seemed laden
with every craving, a craving that had already brought so many
to grief. Terrifying as it was to behold, I was so burdened in
spirit that I lost all hope of scaling the heights.

(*Inferno* I.1–21 and 49–54)

With this, then, comes his descent under the aegis of Virgil as
himself a poet of significant journeying down into the pit, across the
ever narrowing circles of hell reaching down beneath Jerusalem to
the very centre of the earth. There ranged before him, and ever ready
to engage and to be engaged in a dialogue of variously anguished
inspiration, are those who for one reason or another "have lost the
good of the intellect" and who are thus now and forever astray in
respect of their proper humanity: the indifferent and uncommitted
in their insignificant busyness; those unfortunate enough to have
been born either before or beyond the Christian dispensation
(the Dantean Limbo); the intemperate and indulgent (the lustful,
the gluttonous, the hoarders, the prodigal and the inveterately
angry); the violent against their neighbours, against themselves,
against nature and against God; and, way down in the pit,
the fraudulent – the deceivers pure and simple (among them the
flatterers, the traders in civic and clerical office, the hypocrites, the
sowers of discord and the counterfeiters) and, still further down,
the betrayers of trust, the traitors to country, to kindred and to their
lords (including Brutus and Cassius as traitors to Rome and Judas
as traitor to God himself in the person of Christ). God's wrath, to
be sure, is everywhere conspicuous, but deeply woven into the text
and there to be contemplated in the great set-pieces of this first
canticle of the poem is the agony not so much of affliction as of
self-affliction, of the soul's knowing itself only in the catastrophe
of its self-delivery, at which point the ἔσχατος as a matter of what
comes next on the plane, so to speak, of the horizontal is relocated
in the depths, on the plane of the vertical, recognition thus taking
over from retribution as the beginning and end of the soul's now
endless sorrowing.

With what amounts, then, from the point of view of the pilgrim poet to a matter not simply of seeing but of self-seeing, of knowing self in the as yet unresolved substance of its own presence in the world, Dante, still under the wing of Virgil, embarks on the upward way. Again the narrative is energetic, the souls detained for a season on the terraces of Mount Purgatory situated in Dante's imagining of it at the antipodes of Jerusalem seeking in the context of repentance as but a taking into self of the guilt of self to affirm themselves afresh on the plane of properly human loving and thus of properly human being. First then, on the lower slopes of the mountain come the late repentant, the negligent, the indolent and the unshriven, theirs, in the stillness, being a moment of preparation for the rigours of purgatory proper. With purgatory proper, however, stillness gives way to striving as, variously afflicted but committed withal to that same affliction as the way of spiritual renewal, the penitent spirit seeks to affirm the authentic over the inauthentic self on the plane of properly human loving: the proud by way of the boulders they bear on their back, the envious by way of their temporary blindness, the wrathful by way of the stinging smoke of their anger, the slothful by way of an unwonted athleticism, the avaricious and the prodigal by way of their face-down prostration, the gluttonous by way of their emaciation, and the lustful by way of the now purgative fire of their hitherto unbridled passion. And the outcome of it all? In a word, freedom, the freedom to be in keeping with the innermost exigencies of their properly human nature, a freedom enjoyed at last by way of an Edenic peace properly theirs on the summit of the mountain, of the peace, that is to say, properly theirs before the catastrophe of man's first disobedience but awaiting them now as but preliminary in respect of a still more rapturous ascent of the spirit.

Effecting ascents, then, by way of the revised gravity of paradise – of the now upward movement of the spirit as it enters into communion with the One who *is* as of the essence – Dante, committed as he is from this point on to the care of Beatrice as mother, sister, lover, companion and counsellor all rolled into one, proceeds from sphere to sphere there to rejoice with the elect in their own homecoming. First, then, with the heaven of the Moon, the heaven of Mercury and the heaven of Venus, come the hitherto inconstant in their vows, the ambitious for worldly glory and the intemperate in love, souls able now to smile upon what once was but is no longer a way of being. Then, with the heaven of the Sun, come the theological, the philosophical and the mystical spirits, each alike, for all its subsisting as something approaching a species in its own right (the "adeo ut fere quilibet sua propria specie videatur gaudere"of the *De vulgari eloquentia* at I.iii.1), delighting the one in the other as but a parameter of its own existence. In the heaven of Mars, by contrast, we rejoice with those taking up the sword in the name and for the sake of the cross, in the heaven of Jupiter with those who hunger and thirst after righteousness, and in the heaven of Saturn with the contemplative spirits, with those for whom ratiocination is taken up in something closer to consciousness in its pure form. But that is not all, for with his ascent into the heaven of the fixed stars and with his standing now in the presence of the apostles Peter, James and John, Dante, much after the manner of the nervous examinee, is called upon to make his own confession as a wayfaring spirit, to give an account of the faith, of the hope and of the love within him, confession thus understood readying him for the final phase of his journey into God. First, then, as far as that final phase is concerned, and more than ever gracious in its cadencing, comes the prayer, the petitionary utterance placed by Dante upon the lips of his third and final guide Bernard of Clairvaux, the Bernard of the *De diligendo Deo* or *On Loving God*, a prayer enabling him to look at last upon the simple light of the Godhead – simple, to be sure, but by way of perhaps the most exquisite trinitarian formula in the whole of European letters threefold withal in its interleaving of intelligence, love and laughter as but the substance of the One who *is* as of the essence:

> O luce etterna che sola in te sidi,
> sola t'intendi, e da te intelletta
> e intendente te ami e arridi!

O Light Eternal that solely abides in yourself, solely knows yourself, and, by yourself alone understood and understanding, loves and smiles upon yourself!

(*Paradiso* XXXIII.124–26)

But neither is that all, for borne upon the face of the light at once one and three is inscribed, *mirabile dictu*, our likeness, "la nostra effige". How so, Dante wonders, the Godhead, properly speaking, suffering in its simplicity neither differentiation nor addition nor super-inscription, at which point reason, ever honoured by Dante as the in-and-through-which of man's proper operation and thus of his proper coming about as man, is taken up in a love-encompassing constituting both the whereabouts and the first and final cause of his every significant inflexion of the spirit:

> Quella circulazion che sì concetta
> pareva in te come lume reflesso,
> da li occhi miei alquanto circunspetta,
>   dentro da sé, del suo colore stesso,
> mi parve pinta de la nostra effige;
> per che 'l mio viso in lei tutto era messo.
>   Qual è 'l geomètra che tutto s'affige
> per misurar lo cerchio, e non ritrova,
> pensando, quel principio ond' elli indige,
>   tal era io a quella vista nova;
> veder voleva come si convenne
> l'imago al cerchio e come vi s'indova;
>   ma non eran da ciò le proprie penne;
> se non che la mia mente fu percossa
> da un fulgore in che sua voglia venne.
>   A l'alta fantasia qui mancò possa;
> ma già volgeva il mio disio e 'l *velle*,
> sì come rota ch'igualmente è mossa,
>   l'amor che move il sole e l'altre stelle.

That circle, which, thus conceived, appeared in you to be but a reflected light, seemed as I dwelt upon it to bear depicted within itself, in one and the same hue, our likeness, wherefore my sight was wholly set upon it. Like the geometer who, unresting, applies himself to measure the circle, and, for all his thinking, finds not the principle he needs, such was I at that strange sight. I wished to see how the image fitted the circle and was able there to find its place; but for this, were it not that my mind was smitten by a flash whence its wish was fulfilled, my wings were not sufficient. Yet my every power to image forth here failing me, desire and will alike, like a wheel evenly turned, were turned by the love that moves the sun and the other stars.

(*Paradiso* XXXIII.127–45)

JOURNEYING UNDER THE ASPECT OF SEEING: *INFERNO*

To live with the *Inferno* for any length of time, and even more so to encounter it for the first time, is to be impressed by Dante's commitment to the notion – indeed both to the notion and, as Dante sees it, to the sheer artistry – of divine wrath, of God's forever turning back in anger upon the disobedience of mankind as but the first fruits of his creativity. As far, then, as the 'wrath' or retribution moment of the argument is concerned, any number of passages come to mind from the "those dying in the wrath of the Lord" moment of *Inferno* III (the "those" here being the new arrivals in hell):

"Figliuol mio", disse 'l maestro cortese,
"quelli che muoion ne l'ira di Dio
tutti convegnon qui d'ogne paese;
    e pronti sono a trapassar lo rio,
ché la divina giustizia li sprona,
sì che la tema si volve in disio.

Quinci non passa mai anima buona;
e però, se Caron di te si lagna,
ben puoi sapere omai che 'l suo dir suona".

"Those, my son," said my gracious master, "dying in the wrath
of God foregather here from every clime, and, for that divine
justice so spurs them on that fear turns to desire, they are eager
to cross the river. By this way no good spirit ever passes, and
if therefore Charon raises his voice against you, then well you
may understand the burden of what he says."

(*Inferno* III.121–29)

to and beyond the "why are these not further down in the pit"
moment of Canto XI:

Ma dimmi: quei de la palude pingue,
che mena il vento, e che batte la pioggia,
e che s'incontran con sì aspre lingue,
 perché non dentro da la città roggia
sono ei puniti, se Dio li ha in ira?
e se non li ha, perché sono a tal foggia?

But tell me, those of the slimy marsh, those driven by the
tempest, those battered by the rain, and those upon meeting
so ferocious in expression, why, if God's wrath be upon them,
are they not punished within the fiery city? And, if not, why
are they put to such suffering?

(*Inferno* XI.70–75)

while as far as the artistry of it all is concerned we have this from
just a little further down in the pit:

Indi venimmo al fine ove si parte
lo secondo giron dal terzo, e dove
si vede di giustizia orribil arte.

Thus we came to the boundary of the second and the beginning
of the third circle, there to behold the terrifying handiwork
of justice.

(*Inferno* XIV.4–6)

But upon reflection – and here we move and indeed must move
beyond the often enough pedalled but in truth banal interpretation
of Dante in general and of the *Inferno* in particular as but a matter
merely of comeuppance and of this as an occasion for divine
rejoicing – the question arises as to who, precisely, is punishing
whom in this first canticle of the *Commedia*; for while on the
face of it it is indeed a question of God's looking back in anger,
the agony of it all is in truth the agony generated by the soul's
now and forever knowing itself in the delivery of self to the self-
consciously inauthentic project, at which point comeuppance
gives way to ontological catastrophe as the deep substance of
the text. So, for example, the case of Francesca da Rimini among
the *lussuriosi* or intemperate of Canto V, a spirit notable not least
for her graciousness in Dante's regard, for her care and courtesy
in respect of his pausing to speak with her in the midst of her
storm-tossed distress. Almost immediately, however, graciousness
as all of a piece within the complex economy of the whole with
readiness or biddability as a disposition of the spirit gives way to
a movement of self-exoneration, to a carefully considered and in
this case exquisitely orchestrated redistribution of guilt as – here as
throughout in hell – the sole means of standing securely, indeed of
standing at all, in her own presence:

"Amor, ch'al cor gentil ratto s'apprende,
prese costui de la bella persona
che mi fu tolta; e 'l modo ancor m'offende.
Amor, ch'a nullo amato amar perdona,
mi prese del costui piacer sì forte,
che, come vedi, ancor non m'abbandona.
Amor condusse noi ad una morte.

Caina attende chi a vita ci spense".
Queste parole da lor ci fuor porte.

"Love, which quickly lays hold of the noble heart, seized
this one by way of the fair form that was taken from me, the
manner thereof taxing me still. Love, which absolves no one
loved from loving, seized me by way of his comeliness, and this
so strongly that, as you see, it forsakes me not even yet. Love
brought us to one death, Cain awaiting him who quenched
our life." These words were borne to us from them.

(*Inferno* V.100–108)

Dante – meaning by this the Dante-character in the poem – is duly
sympathetic, and indeed moved to tears, as he looks on and listens, but
Dante the author, here as throughout perfectly secure in his sense of
the matter to hand, at once sidesteps strategy in favour of substance, at
which point Francesca – the never less than gracious Francesca – has
nowhere to look other than into the recesses of self there to ponder
yet again the self-apostasy of it all, the delivery of self despite self to its
own undoing. On the one hand, then, the nothing if not devastating
"but tell me" of line 118 with its invitation – but in truth an invitation,
this, leaving no room for manoeuvre – to speak more fully to her case:

> Poi mi rivolsi a loro e parla' io,
> e cominciai: "Francesca, i tuoi martìri
> a lagrimar mi fanno tristo e pio.
> Ma dimmi: al tempo d'i dolci sospiri,
> a che e come concedette amore
> che conosceste i dubbiosi disiri?"

Then, turning to them once more to speak, I began: "Francesca,
your suffering fills me with sadness and compassion to the
point of weeping. But tell me how and by what means it was
that, in the moment of your sweet sighing, love granted you
knowledge of these, your as yet uncertain desires?"

(*Inferno* V.115–20)

while on the other hand the descent into self there to ponder yet again the ontic instant, the moment, that is to say, which in the absence of repentance as but a turning of the spirit lives on to shape and substantiate this or that instance of specifically human being into all eternity:

> E quella a me: "Nessun maggior dolore
> che ricordarsi del tempo felice
> ne la miseria; e ciò sa 'l tuo dottore.
>   Ma s'a conoscer la prima radice
> del nostro amor tu hai cotanto affetto,
> dirò come colui che piange e dice.
>   Noi leggiavamo un giorno per diletto
> di Lancialotto come amor lo strinse;
> soli eravamo e sanza alcun sospetto.
>   Per più fïate li occhi ci sospinse
> quella lettura, e scolorocci il viso;
> ma solo un punto fu quel che ci vinse.
>   Quando leggemmo il disïato riso
> esser basciato da cotanto amante,
> questi, che mai da me non fia diviso,
>   la bocca mi basciò tutto tremante.
> Galeotto fu 'l libro e chi lo scrisse;
> quel giorno più non vi leggemmo avante".
>   Mentre che l'uno spirto questo disse,
> l'altro piangëa; sì che di pietade
> io venni men così com' io morisse.
>   E caddi come corpo morto cade.

And she to me: "There is as your teacher knows full well no greater sorrow than that of recalling in circumstances of wretchedness good times past. But in that you have so great a desire to know of our love's first coming about, I shall speak of it as one who weeps in the very telling of it. One day, for pleasure pure and simple, we read of Lancelot and how he was constrained by love. We were alone and without misgiving.

Often and enough as we read our eyes met and our faces blanched, but one moment alone was it that overcame us. Reading as we did how the longed-for smile was kissed by so great a lover, he who shall never be parted from me kissed my lips all atrembling. A Galeotto was the book and he who wrote it, and that day we read no further in it." While thus one spirit spoke, the other wept such that for pity I myself, as if in death, swooned and fell as a dead body falls.

(*Inferno* V.121–42)

Straightaway, then, on just about the threshold of the canticle, or very soon thereafter, retribution pure and simple as a way of seeing and understanding what is going on in the *Inferno* gives way to something at once morally, intellectually and psychologically wholly more profound, and indeed, existentially speaking, wholly more significant – to, in circumstances of contritionlessness, the agony of self-presencing, of every strategy of self-preservation notwithstanding, knowing self in the now and forever more catastrophic truth of self. And what applies early on in the canticle applies all the way down the line, affliction in hell, and indeed as the very meaning of hell, being a matter of *self*-affliction; so, for example, the case of Pier delle Vigne among the suicides, every attempt to sidestep the guilt of self (always and everywhere in the *Inferno* a necessary but, somewhere in the depths, self-consciously futile gesture) evaporating much after the manner of the morning mist in favour of a stark encounter with self in the innermost parts thereof. The harlot Jealousy notwithstanding, it was, in other words, I – I and no other – who visited the ultimate injustice upon my just self:

> La meretrice che mai da l'ospizio
> di Cesare non torse li occhi putti,
> morte comune e de le corti vizio,
>   infiammò contra me li animi tutti;
> e li 'nfiammati infiammar sì Augusto,
> che 'lieti onor tornaro in tristi lutti.

L'animo mio, per disdegnoso gusto,
credendo col morir fuggir disdegno,
ingiusto fece me contra me giusto.

The harlot that never turned her whorish eyes from Caesar's household – everywhere the death and undoing of courts – inflamed everyone's minds against me, and they, thus inflamed, did so inflame Augustus that the honour in which I delighted gave way to the bitterest of griefs. My mind, scornfully disposed and thinking by death to escape scorn, made me unjust to my just self.

(*Inferno* XIII.64–72)

or, among the false counsellors, Ulysses, where a still heady commitment to the cause as a means of subduing the still small voice of conscience is tinged in the self-same instant by a deeper, insistent and more properly abiding sense of the folly of it all:

"O frati", dissi "che per cento milia
perigli siete giunti a l'occidente,
a questa tanto picciola vigilia
   d'i nostri sensi ch'è del rimanente,
non vogliate negar l'esperïenza,
di retro al sol, del mondo sanza gente.
   Considerate la vostra semenza:
fatti non foste a viver come bruti,
ma per seguir virtute e canoscenza".
   Li miei compagni fec' io sì aguti,
con questa orazion picciola, al cammino,
che a pena poscia li avrei ritenuti;
   e volta nostra poppa nel mattino,
de' remi facemmo ali al folle volo,
sempre acquistando dal lato mancino.

"O brothers," I said, "who through a hundred thousand perils have reached the west, to this so brief vigil of the senses that remains to us choose not to deny experience, in the sun's track, of the unpeopled world. Take thought of the seed from which you spring. You were not born to live as brutes, but to follow virtue and knowledge." With these brief words I so fired up my companions for the voyage that thereafter I could scarce rein them in, and so with our poop towards morning we made of our oars wings for the foolish flight, gaining always on the left.

(*Inferno* XXVI.112–26)

True, the agony of self-presencing seems elsewhere in the *Inferno* to be less insistent, the aforementioned strategies of self-preservation – to wit *frantic self-exoneration* and *loud proclamation* – serving to deflect or to disguise the sensation of guilt; but that precisely is the point, the strategies of self-preservation only ever serving – as in a moment of stillness the troubled spirit understands only too well – to deepen and to refine its suffering.

This, then, from the point of view of the pilgrim spirit here and now, for those, that is to say, with time still for the amendment of life, is what it means to speak of hell as but a matter of *seeing* or of *self-confrontation*. For those, in other words, with time still for the amendment of life it is a question of lingering for a season on the plane of self-recognition, of the kind of self-knowing indispensable within the economy of the whole to anything approaching resurrection on the plane of properly human being. Now this by no means does away with the 'wrath of God' and retribution component of the *Inferno*, these things between them being taken up, however, in a discourse more properly analytical in kind, more properly attuned to the notion of indictment as a matter withal of *self*-indictment.

JOURNEYING UNDER THE ASPECT OF STRIVING: *PURGATORIO*

The *Purgatorio* – the beautiful *Purgatorio* – is on the face of it, and indeed in very truth, a meditation on the *reatus poenae* or 'debt of punishment' understood by the theologians to be incurred by sin as duly repented and absolved but entailing even so a debt to be paid off, a period of penitential suffering as the condition of the soul's coming home fully and finally to the company of the elect; so, for example, these lines from the final pages of the Thomist *Summa theologiae* on purgatory as, precisely, a matter of settling the score hereafter and on this as an article of faith:

Respondeo dicendum quod ex illis quae supra determinata sunt, satis potest constare purgatorium esse post hanc vitam. Si enim, per contritionem deleta culpa, non tollitur ex reatus poenae, nec etiam se, per venialis, dimissis mortalibus tolluntur, et iustitia Dei hoc exigit et peccatum per poenam debitam ordinetur, oportet quod illi qui post contritionem de peccato decedit et absolutionem, ante satisfactionem debitam quod post hanc vitam puniatur. Et ideo illi qui purgatorium negant, contra divinam iustitiam loquuntur. Et propter hoc erroneum est, et a fide alienum. Unde Gregorius Nyssenus post praedicta verba subiungit: *Hoc praedicamus dogma veritatis servantes et ita credimus.* Hoc enim universalis Ecclesia tenet, *pro defunctis exorans ut a peccatis solvantur,* quod non potest nisi de illis qui sunt in purgatorio intelligi. Ecclesiae autem auctoritati quicumque resistit haeresim incurrit.

I answer that from the conclusions we have drawn above it is sufficiently clear that there is a purgatory after this life. For if the debt of punishment is not paid in full after the stain of sin has been washed away by contrition (for again venial sin is not always removed with the remission of mortal sin), it follows that he who after contrition and absolution for his sin nonetheless dies without making due satisfaction should properly be punished in the life to come. Wherefore those who deny purgatory speak against the justice of God, for which reason their contention is erroneous and contrary to faith. Hence Gregory of Nyssa, after the words quoted above, adds: "This we preach holding to the teaching of truth, and such is our belief." This the universal Church holds, namely that "by praying for the dead that they may be loosed from sins", something which cannot be understood except as referring to purgatory. Whosoever therefore resists the authority of the Church incurs a note of heresy.

(*Summa theologiae* IIIa, app. I (*Quaestio de Purgatorio*), art. 1 resp.)

Thus far, then, Dante is all of a mind with the theologians, his too being a sense of purgatory as, whatever else it is, a matter of making satisfaction. True, there is both in practice and in principle rather more to it than this, for if indeed it is a question of making satisfaction then by the same token it is a question of doing so in the context (*a*) of a species of stillness and of sorrowing reaching down into the recesses of self, the stillness and sorrowing of radical self-confrontation, and (*b*) of faith in the wideness of God's mercy; so, for example, Manfred's confession in Canto III with its nuancing of the at once psychological and theological issue here in precisely this sense:

> Poi sorridendo disse: "Io son Manfredi,
> nepote di Costanza imperadrice;
> ond' io ti priego che, quando tu riedi,
>   vadi a mia bella figlia, genitrice
> de l'onor di Cicilia e d'Aragona,
> e dichi 'l vero a lei, s'altro si dice.
>   Poscia ch'io ebbi rotta la persona
> di due punte mortali, io mi rendei,
> piangendo, a quei che volontier perdona.
>   Orribil furon li peccati miei;
> ma la bontà infinita ha sì gran braccia,
> che prende ciò che si rivolge a lei".

Then said he, smiling: "I am Manfred, grandson of the Empress Constance. Therefore I beg of you that when you return you go to my fair daughter, mother of the pride of Sicily and of

Aragon, and speak to the truth should another tale be told. After I had my body cleft by two mortal strokes I gave myself up with tears to him who freely pardons; horrible were my sins, but the infinite goodness has arms so wide that it receives whoever turns to it."

(*Purgatorio* III.112–23)

But that notwithstanding, it is indeed a question in this second canticle of the *Commedia* of satisfaction, of making good as a prior and necessary condition of the soul's ultimate emergence; so, for example, these lines from Cantos X and XI of the *Purgatorio*, the pride cantos of the text, explicit when it comes to purgatory as, whatever else it is, a matter of squaring the account beyond the bar:

> Non vo' però, lettor, che tu ti smaghi
> di buon proponimento per udire
> come Dio vuol che 'l debito si paghi.
> ...
> "Io sono Omberto; e non pur a me danno
> superbia fa, ché tutti miei consorti
> ha ella tratti seco nel malanno.
> E qui convien ch'io questo peso porti
> per lei, tanto che a Dio si sodisfaccia,
> poi ch'io nol fe' tra ' vivi, qui tra ' morti".
> ...
> "Quelli è", rispuose, "Provenzan Salvani;
> ed è qui perché fu presuntüoso
> a recar Siena tutta a le sue mani.
> Ito è così e va, sanza riposo,
> poi che morì; cotal moneta rende
> a sodisfar chi è di là troppo oso".

I would not, indeed, reader, that, hearing how God wishes the debt to be paid, you be turned aside from your good purpose ... "I am Omberto, and am not alone among my kinsfolk as a victim of pride, for they all of them have been dragged down

by it. Here then, among the dead – since I did it not among
the living – must I bear this burden for it, until such time
as God be satisfied" … "That," he answered, "is Provenzan
Salvani, and he is here because he presumed to hold all Siena
in his hands. Thus he has gone, and goes still, without respite
from the day of his death, such being the coin everyone too
bold there below pays by way of making good."

(Purgatorio X.106–108, XI.67–72 and 121–26)

But the 'whatever else it is' moment of the argument is, in fact,
all-important, for what we have in the *Purgatorio*, over and above
its transactional component, is yet again something morally,
theologically and existentially wholly more significant; for what we
have here is a meditation upon what within the figural economy
of the text as a whole amounts to a sense of purgatory as but a
further phase of man's proper journeying here and now, upon the
kind of spiritual discipline whereby, in and through what amounts
to an assiduous process of love-organization under the conditions
of time and space, the individual seeks to free self for his or her
blessed ulteriority, for all that he or she has it in self to be and to
become as a creature of moral, intellectual and, as the deep and
abiding substance of these things, eschatological accountability.
On the one hand, then, there is the love-organization aspect
of the argument, its secure sense of human experience properly
understood as but a matter of love-harvesting, of bringing home
the contingent to the connatural on the plane of properly human
desiring:

> "Né creator né creatura mai",
> cominciò el, "figliuol, fu sanza amore,
> o naturale o d'animo; e tu 'l sai.
> Lo naturale è sempre sanza errore,
> ma l'altro puote errar per malo obietto
> o per troppo o per poco di vigore.
> Mentre ch'elli è nel primo ben diretto,

e ne' secondi sé stesso misura,
esser non può cagion di mal diletto;
  ma quando al mal si torce, o con più cura
o con men che non dee corre nel bene,
contra 'l fattore adovra sua fattura".

He began: "Neither Creator nor creature, my son, was – as well you know – ever without love, either natural or elective. Natural love can never err, but the other may in respect either of an unworthy object or else by way either of excess or defect. So long as it is directed on the highest good and as regards all others is properly proportionate, it cannot be the cause of doubtful pleasure. But bent upon evil or chasing the good with more or less zeal than it ought, against the creator works his creature."

(*Purgatorio* XVII.91–102)

while on the other, and constituting the final cause or point of arrival of love-harvesting thus understood, there is the emancipation aspect of the argument as registered both on the threshold of the canticle and again – and not without the most far-reaching of theological and (more especially) ecclesiological implications – towards the end thereof:

Or ti piaccia gradir la sua venuta:
libertà va cercando, ch'è sì cara,
come sa chi per lei vita rifiuta
    …
Non aspettar mio dir più né mio cenno;
libero, dritto e sano è tuo arbitrio,
e fallo fora non fare a suo senno:
    per ch'io te sovra te corono e mitrio.

May it please you to be gracious to his coming. He goes seeking liberty, which is so dear, as he knows who gives his life for it … No longer expect word or sign from me. Free, upright and whole is your will and it were a fault not to act upon its bidding; therefore over yourself I crown and mitre you.

(*Purgatorio* I.70–72 and XXVII.139–42)

But to this we need by way of honouring the substance, not to say the seriousness, of Dante's discourse hereabouts to stress once more the arduousness of it all, for when it comes to bringing home the lesser to the greater on the plane of properly human loving there is nothing facile about it, nothing by way of easy accomplishment. On the contrary, the pain of purgatory is absolute, absolute to the point of breaking the most resolute of pilgrim spirits; so for example, on the terrace of the proud, these words placed by Dante upon the lips of the pilgrim poet as he looks on, words authorized from out of the depths of his own purgatorial existence:

> Come per sostentar solaio o tetto,
> per mensola talvolta una figura
> si vede giugner le ginocchia al petto,
> la qual fa del non ver vera rancura
> nascere 'n chi la vede; così fatti
> vid' io color, quando puosi ben cura.
> Vero è che più e meno eran contratti
> secondo ch'avien più e meno a dosso;
> e qual più pazïenza avea ne li atti,
> piangendo parea dicer: 'Più non posso'.

As from time to time we see for the purposes of supporting a ceiling or a roof a figure with its knees drawn up to its chest, a figure engendering in its unreality a real sense of distress in those looking on, that is how, I myself looking on attentively, saw those now before me. Bent double they were indeed according to the greater or lesser weight on their back, those showing forth the greatest forbearance seeming amid their tears to say "Alas, I can no more."

(*Purgatorio* X.130–39)

True, suffering here coincides within the again complex economy of it all with solace – Dante's point precisely in the twenty-third canto of the text where by way of those words placed upon the lips of Forese Donati among the gluttonous on the sixth terrace of the mountain he summons up the notion of Christ's going gladly to the cross as the way of universal emancipation:

> Tutta esta gente che piangendo canta
> per seguitar la gola oltra misura,
> in fame e 'n sete qui si rifà santa.
>   Di bere e di mangiar n'accende cura
> l'odor ch'esce del pomo e de lo sprazzo
> che si distende su per sua verdura.
>   E non pur una volta, questo spazzo
> girando, si rinfresca nostra pena;
> io dico pena, e dovria dir sollazzo,
>   ché quella voglia a li alberi ci mena
> che menò Cristo lieto a dire 'Elì',
> quando ne liberò con la sua vena.

All these who weep as they sing, having followed their appetite beyond measure, regain here, in hunger and thirst, their righteousness. The fragrance emanating from the fruit and from the spray and dispersed over its verdure kindles in us a craving to eat and to drink, and not once only is our pain renewed as we circle this space. I say pain but ought to say solace, for to the tree we are led by that will which led Christ gladly to say "*Elì*" when with his own veins he freed us.

(*Purgatorio* XXIII.64–75)

But solace notwithstanding, the agony of it all is intense, there being no softening of the "Alas, I can no longer" of the purgatorial way proper, of the grim countenance, nay of the grim substance, of love-harvesting as the in-and-through-which of new life. This, then, from the point of view of the pilgrim spirit here and now, for those, that is to say, with time still for the amendment of life, is what it means to speak of purgatory as but a matter of *striving* or of *self-reconfiguration*. For those, in other words, with time still for the amendment of life it is a question of the kind of love-emancipation making for – as Dante himself puts it in this second canticle of the poem – the 'butterfly' emergence of the spirit in its now and henceforth soaring substance. But neither here does this mean doing away with the *reatus poenae* or 'debt of punishment' component of the argument, but rather its taking up in a discourse of more immediate concern, in a discourse, that is to say, more properly attuned to the struggle always and everywhere verifiable in human experience to affirm self over self in the name and for the sake of an authentic act of specifically human being.

JOURNEYING UNDER THE ASPECT OF SURPASSING:
PARADISO

With the *Paradiso* – the sublime *Paradiso* – we come to Dante's celebration of what he himself sees as the taking up of man's 'humanity' as man in the kind of 'transhumanity' as, again, but the most immanent of its immanent possibilities, and this by way of the 'elevating grace' or *gratia elevans* whereby he himself is lifted to and confirmed in his proper ulteriority as a creature of seeing, understanding and desiring. And here the pilgrim poet's gratitude knows no bounds, his, at every stage along the way, being a hymn to the grace from on high whereby he is confirmed in an ever more ample species both of knowing and of loving; so for example, by way of an act of thanksgiving making in its intensity for an eclipse even of Beatrice herself, these lines from Canto X:

> E Bëatrice cominciò: "Ringrazia,
> ringrazia il Sol de li angeli, ch'a questo
> sensibil t'ha levato per sua grazia".
>   Cor di mortal non fu mai sì digesto
> a divozione e a rendersi a Dio
> con tutto 'l suo gradir cotanto presto,
>   come a quelle parole mi fec' io;

e sì tutto 'l mio amore in lui si mise,
che Bëatrice eclissò ne l'oblio.

And Beatrice began: "Give thanks, give thanks to the Sun of
the angels who by grace has lifted you to such beholding."
Never was mortal heart so intent upon devotion and so swift
in – as its every delight – making itself over to God as I upon
hearing those words. Indeed, so completely was my love set
upon him that Beatrice herself was by its forgetfulness eclipsed.

(*Paradiso* X.52–60)

or the 'burnt offering of gratitude' moment of Canto XIV
consequent on yet a still more blessed translation of the spirit:

Quindi ripreser li occhi miei virtute
a rilevarsi; e vidimi translato
sol con mia donna in più alta salute.
Ben m'accors' io ch'io era più levato,
per l'affocato riso de la stella,
che mi parea più roggio che l'usato.
Con tutto 'l core e con quella favella
ch'è una in tutti, a Dio feci olocausto,
qual conveniesi a la grazia novella.

From this my eyes recovered strength enough to look up once
more, and, alone with my lady, I beheld myself translated
to still greater bliss. Well assured was I of my ascent by the
enkindled smile of the star, fiery it seemed to me, beyond
its wont, whereupon with all my heart and in the language
thereof common to one and all I made unto God a holocaust
such as befitted this further grace.

(*Paradiso* XIV.82–90)

or, from the now climactic phase of the poem, the 'grace abounding'
sequence of Canto XXXIII, grace once again vouchsafing a moment
of spiritual intelligence at the far limits thereof:

Oh abbondante grazia ond' io presunsi
ficcar lo viso per la luce etterna,
tanto che la veduta vi consunsi!
 Nel suo profondo vidi che s'interna,
legato con amore in un volume,
ciò che per l'universo si squaderna:
 sustanze e accidenti e lor costume
quasi conflati insieme, per tal modo
che ciò ch'i' dico è un semplice lume.
 La forma universal di questo nodo
credo ch'i' vidi, perché più di largo,
dicendo questo, mi sento ch'i' godo.

Oh grace abounding whereby I presumed to fix my look
on the eternal light such that I saw at the far limits of my
seeing! I saw enclosed in its depths, bound up with love in
one volume, everything unfolded leaf by leaf throughout the
universe: substance and accidents and their modalities, fused,
as it were, one with another such that what I speak of is but a
simple light. And of this singularity I believe I saw then the
universal form, for in the very telling of it I feel the increase
of my joy.

(*Paradiso* XXXIII.82–93)

But here again we are far from home in respect of what actually is
going on here and what matters about all this; for just as retribution
pure and simple leaves us at a distance from the still centre of Dante's
discourse in the *Inferno*, and just as the paying off of debts leaves
us on the outer edges of his discourse in the *Purgatorio*, so grace as
but an extrinsic or adventitious principle of properly human being
and becoming leaves us in the mere environs of his discourse in the
Paradiso, in the mere vicinity of what he has in mind and indeed of
what he is actually saying here in this third canticle of the poem.
For while indeed grace is both in essence and by definition an
incoming principle of man's proper activity as man it is withal, for
Dante, an inwardly operative principle of that activity, that whereby

nature is quickened and sustained in respect of its proper power to self-transcendence. Typically, in other words, grace, in Dante, is that whereby nature – meaning by this the customary processes of seeing and understanding – is confirmed in its equality to the matter in hand, co-adequated in respect of its high calling; so for example, from early on in the canticle, the "from peak to peak of understanding" passage of Canto IV, grace here functioning as that whereby nature knows itself in its endless exponentiality, in the *can do* (the "giugner puollo" of line 128) of its proper presence and its proper operation in the world:

> "O amanza del primo amante, o diva",
> diss' io appresso, "il cui parlar m'inonda
> e scalda sì, che più e più m'avviva,
> non è l'affezion mia tanto profonda,
> che basti a render voi grazia per grazia;
> ma quei che vede e puote a ciò risponda.
> Io veggio ben che già mai non si sazia
> nostro intelletto, se 'l ver non lo illustra
> di fuor dal qual nessun vero si spazia.
> Posasi in esso, come fera in lustra,
> tosto che giunto l'ha; e giugner puollo:
> se non, ciascun disio sarebbe *frustra*.
> Nasce per quello, a guisa di rampollo,
> a piè del vero il dubbio; ed è natura
> ch'al sommo pinge noi di collo in collo".

"O beloved of the first lover, o divine one," said I then, "whose speech so floods and warms me such that I am ever more quickened, my affection for all its depth is scarce sufficient to render you grace for grace; but may he who sees and can indeed do so answer thereunto. Well do I see that never can our intellect be wholly satisfied unless there shine on it that truth beyond which no truth extends. Therein it rests, as a wild beast in his lair, so soon as it has reached it; and reach it it can, else every desire would be in vain. Our questioning thus

springs up like a shoot at the foot of the truth, nature itself
thus peak by peak urging us on to the summit."

(*Paradiso* IV.118–32)

to which, as likewise eloquent in its sense of nature as not so much
supplemented as strengthened by grace, we may add the "I myself
changing" passage of Canto XXXIII:

> Non perché più ch'un semplice sembiante
> fosse nel vivo lume ch'io mirava,
> che tal è sempre qual s'era davante;
>   ma per la vista che s'avvalorava
> in me guardando, una sola parvenza,
> mutandom' io, a me si travagliava.

Not that the living light upon which I gazed had more than a
single aspect, for ever it remained as it was before; but by my
sight gaining strength as I looked on, the as yet undifferentiated
appearance – I myself changing – was for me transformed.

(*Paradiso* XXXIII.109–14)

If, then, to this we add the vocabulary of self-transcendence (the
"dilatarsi", the "farsi più grande", the "uscire di sé stesso" and the
"sormontar di sopr' a mia virtute" of *Paradiso* XXIII and XXX) then
we have a nothing if not sturdy invitation to interpret the *Paradiso*
as yet a further essay in the deep and abiding viability of the human
project precisely as such, in – for Dante and always and everywhere
by grace – the in some sense and in some degree equality of the
creature to the creator as its proper privilege and patrimony.

    This, then, from the point of view of the pilgrim spirit here and
now, for those, that is to say, with time still for the amendment
of life, is what it means to speak of paradise as but a matter of
surpassing or of *self-transcendence*. For those, in other words, with
time still for the amendment of life it is a question of the kind
of ecstatic resolution awaiting as its *terminus ad quem* or point of

arrival every significant inflexion of the spirit on the planes both of understanding and of desiring. Now grace, to be sure, abounds as the *sine qua non* of resolution thus understood, as, more exactly, that whereby man as man is raised up and freshly empowered in respect of an ever more exalted species of knowing and loving. But that, precisely, is the point, for it is a question here not merely, indeed not at all, of the *superadditional*, of, in respect of man's connatural power to seeing, understanding and choosing, grace as *brought to bear*, but rather of a mutual indwelling of the divine and of the human initiative at the still centre of personality making for the co-adequation or making equal of the one who says 'I' to his or her coming forth on the plane of properly human being.

FIVE

The Power of the Word: Issues in the Area of Language and Literature

B EING, BECOMING AND THE sanctity of the word – the triumph of the image.

BEING, BECOMING AND THE SANCTITY OF THE WORD

Both implicitly and explicitly Dante's is a preoccupation with the nature and function of the word as that whereby the individual or group of individuals stands securely in his, her or their own presence, and this both in its inception and in its relativity under the conditions of time and space. As regards, then, its inception, it is a question, he thinks, of the language given with creation itself, a language fully formed lexically, morphologically and phonologically, and coming down by way of the sons of Heber into the time of Christ as the language of grace:

> Redeuntes igitur ad propositum, dicimus certam formam
> locutionis a Deo cum anima prima concreatam fuisse. Dico
> autem 'formam' et quantum ad rerum vocabula et quantum
> ad vocabulorum constructionem et quantum ad constructionis
> prolationem ... Hac forma locutionis locutus est Adam; hac
> forma locutionis locuti sunt omnes posteri eius usque ad
> edificationem turris Babel, que 'turris confusionis' interpretatur;
> hanc formam locutionis hereditati sunt filii Heber, qui ab
> eo dicti sunt Hebrei. Hiis solis post confusionem remansit,
> ut Redemptor noster, qui ex illis oriturus erat secundum

humanitatem, non lingua confusionis, sed gratie frueretur. Fuit ergo hebraicum ydioma illud quod primi loquentis labia fabricarunt.

Returning, then, to my subject, I say that a certain form of language was created by God along with the first soul. I say 'form' with reference both to the words used for things and to the morphology and inflexion of those words ... This was the form of speech used by Adam and by all his descendants until the building of the Tower of Babel, which, being interpreted, means the 'tower of confusion', and it was inherited by the sons of Heber who from him were called Hebrews. They alone retained it after the confusion, so that our redeemer, who was to be born from them according to his humanity, should speak the language not of confusion, but that of grace. So the Hebrew language was the language fashioned upon the lips of the first man to speak.

(De vulgari eloquentia I.vi.4–7)

Prominent already in this passage, however, is the notion of disruption and of diaspora, of the linguistic chaos visited upon man by God in consequence of his continuing disobedience, of most conspicuously his effrontery in seeking by way of a tower of monstrous proportion not merely to equal but to surpass his maker. Thereafter, and indeed as an immediate consequence of Babel, it was, Dante explains, a question of linguistic otherness, and indeed not merely of otherness but of barbarity, of a more or less complete falling away from the pristine grace and excellence of what, linguistically, once was. As far, however, as the *De vulgari eloquentia* itself is concerned, it is at this point – at the point of linguistic diversity as but a product of man's now more than ever fragile relationship with his maker – that evolution takes over from catastrophe as a way of seeing and understanding the linguistic issue both in its diachronic and in its synchronic aspects, in respect, that is to say, both of its development along the axis of time and of its complexion at any given point along the way. Gradually emerging as the argument goes on, in other words, and doubtless present to Dante as he looks on as an occasion both for sadness and for misgiving, is a sense of the shifting substance of everything subject to man's *beneplacitum* or say so, of, in short, cultural relativity as always and everywhere the way of it under the conditions of time and space. Discernible already in the *Convivio*, then, where it is a question of comparing the nobility of Latin and the vernacular precisely under this aspect, is an albeit as yet lightly figured strain of melancholy as Dante contemplates over and against the stability of the former the *in*stability of the latter, the forces of generation and decay making over time for a just about total eclipse of the old by the new:

Onde vedemo ne le scritture antiche de le comedie e tragedie latine, che non si possono transmutare, quello medesimo che oggi avemo; che non avviene del volgare, lo quale a piacimento artificiato si transmuta. Onde vedemo ne le cittadi d'Italia, se bene volemo agguardare, da cinquanta anni in qua molti vocabuli essere spenti e nati e variati; onde se 'l picciol tempo così transmuta, molto più transmuta lo maggiore. Sì ch'io dico, che se coloro che partiron d'esta vita già sono mille anni tornassero a le loro cittadi, crederebbero la loro cittade essere occupata da gente strana, per la lingua da loro discordante. Di questo si parlerà altrove più compiutamente in uno libello ch'io intendo di fare, Dio concedente, di Volgare Eloquenza.

Consequently, we find in the ancient Latin comedies and tragedies, which cannot suffer change, a form of language identical with that used today, something that cannot be said of the vernacular, which is made over again in accordance with changes in taste. And so, were we to examine the matter carefully, we would find that in the cities of Italy in the course of the last fifty years many words have become extinct, have been born or have undergone change; and if just a little time has brought about all this change, so much more will a longer one have done so. Indeed I am quite sure that if those who departed this life a thousand years ago were to return to their native cities, they would think them occupied by a foreign race, so much does today's language differ from theirs – a topic, this, of which I will speak more fully elsewhere, in a little book I have it in mind to write, God willing, on *Eloquence in the Vernacular*.

(*Convivio* I.v.8–10)

– while in the *De vulgari eloquentia* itself we have these lines likewise attuned to the notion of language in at any rate its post-Babelic aspect as but a matter of – like everything else subject to human determination – coming and going with the passage of time:

Dicimus ergo quod nullus effectus superat suam causam, in quantum effectus est, quia nil potest efficere quod non est. Cum igitur omnis nostra loquela – preter illam homini primo concreatam a Deo – sit a nostro beneplacito reparata post confusionem illam que nil aliud fuit quam prioris oblivio, et homo sit instabilissimum atque variabilissimum animal, nec durabilis nec continua esse potest, sed sicut alia que nostra sunt, puta mores et habitus, per locorum temporumque distantias variari oportet ... Quapropter audacter testamur quod si vetustissimi Papienses nunc resurgerent, sermone vario vel diverso cum modernis Papiensibus loquerentur ... Si ergo per eandem gentem sermo variatur, ut dictum est, successive per tempora, nec stare ullo modo potest, necesse est ut disiunctim abmotimque morantibus varie varietur, ceu varie variantur mores et habitus, qui nec natura nec consortio confirmantur, sed humanis beneplacitis localique congruitate nascuntur.

We say that no effect is more powerful than its cause, insofar as it is an effect, since nothing can bring about or produce that which itself it is not. And since, therefore, every language of man, except that which was created by God for and with the first man, has been restored to suit our pleasure after that confusion which was nothing but a forgetting of the former speech; and since, moreover, man is a most unstable and changeable animal and his language cannot be lasting or constant but must vary according to times and places as do other human things such as manners and customs, I do not think that there should be any doubt that language varies with time ... Thus we may confidently declare that were the most ancient inhabitants of Pavia to return to life, they would speak a language very different from that of the modern inhabitants thereof ... If therefore the language of one people gradually varies as we have said over the years, and can in no way remain stabilized, it must of necessity vary when people live separated and far from one another, just as those manners and customs vary that are not regulated by nature or by agreement, but simply by people's tastes and local conformity.

(De vulgari eloquentia I.ix.6–7 and 10)

– lines to which we need for the record to add the following from the final moments of Canto XXVI of the *Paradiso*, a passage that, while revising the linguistic schedule of the earlier text (the original Hebraic tongue was now long spent by the time we reach Babel), confirms the *ad placitum* moment of the argument, the notion, that is to say, of language in its precise form as but a matter of passing pleasure:

> La lingua ch'io parlai fu tutta spenta
> innanzi che a l'ovra inconsummabile
> fosse la gente di Nembròt attenta:
>   ché nullo effetto mai razïonabile,
> per lo piacere uman che rinovella
> seguendo il cielo, sempre fu durabile.
>   Opera naturale è ch'uom favella;
> ma così o così, natura lascia
> poi fare a voi secondo che v'abbella.
>   Pria ch'i' scendessi a l'infernale ambascia,
> I s'appellava in terra il sommo bene

onde vien la letizia che mi fascia;
  e El si chiamò poi: e ciò convene,
ché l'uso d'i mortali è come fronda
in ramo, che sen va e altra vene.

The tongue I spoke was all extinct before Nimrod's race gave
their mind to the unaccomplishable task; for since human
choice is renewed with the course of heaven no product
whatever of reason can last forever. It is a work of nature that
man should speak, but whether in this way or that nature then
leaves you to follow your own pleasure. Before I descended
to the anguish of hell the Supreme Good from whom comes
the joy that swathes me about was named *I* on earth, and later
he was called *El*; and that is fitting, for the usage of mortals is
like a leaf on a branch, which goes and another comes.

(*Paradiso* XXVI.124–38)

But with what in this sense amounts to an again melancholy account
of language in its ever changing complexion, its long since having
left behind the language of grace given with the act itself of existence, we are as yet far off when it comes to the nub of the issue in
Dante; for in Dante language enters as of the essence into the ontological economy of the whole. Far from subsisting, in other words,
as a mere tool of specifically human being or means of transacting
this or that item of everyday business, it constitutes, if not the intelligible form of that being, then the principle at least of its actuality
and accessibility. Already, then, in the *Convivio* there is a sense of
language – of in this case, Dante's beloved *lingua di sì* – as the ground
and guarantee of his own first and second "perfection", of his own
being and *being well*, at which point not merely the sacramentality
but the sacredness of language as a principle – as *the* principle – of
man's proper coming about as man and thus of his standing securely
in his own presence commends itself as a cause for rejoicing:

Onde con ciò sia cosa che due perfezioni abbia l'uomo, una
prima e una seconda (la prima lo fa essere, la seconda lo fa

essere buono), se la propria loquela m'è stata cagione e de
l'una e de l'altra, grandissimo beneficio da lei ho ricevuto.
E ch'ella sia stata a me d'essere [cagione, e ancora di buono
essere] se per me non stesse, brievemente si può mostrare.
Non è [inconveniente] a una cosa esser più cagioni efficienti,
avvegna che una sia massima de l'altre; onde lo fuoco e
lo martello sono cagioni efficienti de lo coltello, avvegna
che massimamente è il fabbro. Questo mio volgare fu
congiugnitore de li miei generanti, che con esso parlavano, sì
come 'l fuoco è disponitore del ferro al fabbro che fa lo coltello;
per che manifesto è lui essere concorso a la mia generazione,
e così essere alcuna cagione del mio essere. Ancora, questo
mio volgare fu introduttore di me ne la via di scienza, che è
ultima perfezione, in quanto con esso io entrai ne lo latino e
con esso mi fu mostrato: lo quale latino poi mi fu via a più
innanzi andare. E così è palese, e per me conosciuto, esso
essere stato a me grandissimo benefattore. Anche, è stato
meco d'uno medesimo studio, e ciò posso così mostrare.
Ciascuna cosa studia naturalmente a la sua conservazione:
onde, se lo volgare per sé studiare potesse, studierebbe a
quella; e quella sarebbe, acconciare sé a più stabilitade, e più
stabilitade non potrebbe avere che in legar sé con numero
e con rime. E questo medesimo studio è stato mio, sì come
tanto è palese che non dimanda testimonianza. Per che uno
medesimo studio è stato lo suo e 'l mio; per che di questa
concordia l'amistà è confermata e accresciuta. Anche c'è stata
la benivolenza de la consuetudine, ché dal principio de la mia
vita ho avuta con esso benivolenza e conversazione, e usato
quello diliberando, interpetrando e questionando. Per che, se
l'amistà s'accresce per la consuetudine, sì come sensibilmente
appare, manifesto è che essa in me massimamente è cresciuta,
che sono con esso volgare tutto mio tempo usato. E così
si vede essere a questa amistà concorse tutte le cagioni
generative e accrescitive de l'amistade: per che si conchiude
che non solamente amore, ma perfettissimo amore sia quello
ch'io a lui debbo avere e ho.

Since therefore man may have two perfections, a first and a second perfection, the first causing him to be and the second to be well, then in that my own language has been to me the cause both of the one and of the other I have received from it the greatest benefit. And that it has indeed been the cause both of my being and of my being well can readily and without ado be demonstrated. For while it is possible for a thing to have several efficient causes, only one of them is pre-eminent; so, for example, both the fire and the hammer are efficient causes of the blade, although only the smith is in the fullest sense. Since then, much like the fire that prepares the iron for the smith, this vernacular of mine, being the language my parents spoke, brought them together, it is clear that in thus helping to bring about my birth it was to that extent responsible for my being. Moreover, this same vernacular of mine, inasmuch as by it I came early on to Latin and to an understanding of that language (this thereafter being the means of my further progress), set me on the road to knowledge as but our greatest perfection. It is clear therefore, and something I gladly acknowledge, that this very vernacular has been a wonderful benefactor to me. Furthermore, and as the following makes plain, we have together sought the same goal. For in that everything that *is* naturally seeks to preserve its own being, then if this vernacular were able to search out a goal this would be it, namely the greatest possible stability for itself – a stability open to accomplishment by way only of its binding up through rhyme and number. And this precisely has been my own aim, something so obvious as to need no proof. Both of us then have sought out the same goal, and by way of this cooperation our friendship has been strengthened and deepened. Not only that, but between us there has long been good will, for from early on we have enjoyed both fellowship and conversation, the vernacular having throughout been with me in all my deliberation, interpretation and enquiry; wherefore if as by experience we know to be the case friendship seasons over time then this, supremely, has been my own case, this language of mine having been my constant concern. Clearly, then, everything making both for the coming about and for the deepening of friendship has fashioned my own friendship with the vernacular, for which reason, when it comes to debts incurred, it is a matter not merely of love pure and simple but of love at the far limits thereof, and that indeed is how it should be.

(*Convivio* I.xiii.3–10)

True, the passage comes round quickly to the notion of Latin as the way of yet a further perfection, Latin, Dante says, setting him on the road to knowledge as our greatest good. But here we need a distinction, a subtle distinction to be sure, but nonetheless a distinction; for when it comes to Latin and to the Latin *auctores* it is a question of high-cultural consciousness, of a refinement of the spirit there certainly to be celebrated but – or so this passage would seem to suggest – not necessarily, and indeed not at all, at the expense of the vernacularity of his being precisely as such, of its vernacular inception, its vernacular formation and its vernacular substance. And it is this sense of the vernacularity both of his own and of his fellow citizens and compatriots in the world that takes us to the heart of Dante's discourse in both the first and the second books of the *De vulgari eloquentia*; for here in the *De vulgari eloquentia* it is a question, precisely, of the vernacular – or more exactly of the vernacular as confirmed in its now fourfold "illustrious, cardinal, aulic and curial" perfection (Dante's *illustre*) – (*a*) as that whereby this or that group of people at this or that stage in their socio-political, cultural and economic development know themselves and are in turn known in the unique complexion of their presence in the world, and (*b*) as that whereby this or that would-be poet in the *illustre*, having served his apprenticeship in the ways and means of romance-vernacular versemaking, rejoices in the now and henceforth soaring substance of self, in his status as beloved of the gods. On the one hand, then, we have the "simple sign" passage of the first book of the *De vulgari eloquentia*, a passage turning precisely upon the notion of the aforesaid *illustre* as that whereby a new Latin race indeed knows itself and is known in its proper *latinitas*, in its unique civility and spirituality:

Quapropter in actionibus nostris, quantumcunque dividantur in species, hoc signum inveniri oportet quo et ipse mensurentur. Nam, in quantum simpliciter ut homines agimus, virtutem habemus (ut generaliter illam intelligamus); nam secundum ipsam bonum et malum hominem iudicamus; in quantum ut homines cives agimus, habemus legem, secundum quam dicitur civis bonus et malus; in quantum ut homines latini agimus, quedam habemus simplicissima signa et morum et habituum et locutionis, quibus latine actiones ponderantur et mensurantur. Que quidem nobilissima sunt earum que Latinorum sunt actiones, hec nullius civitatis Ytalie propria sunt, et in omnibus comunia sunt: inter que nunc potest illud discerni vulgare quod superius venabamur, quod in qualibet redolet civitate nec cubat in ulla.

Therefore, in our actions, into however many types they may be divided, we must seek out that standard by which they are all to be measured; for insofar as we act simply as human beings we have – as understood in its general sense – virtue according to which we judge a man good or bad; while insofar as, in our capacity as human beings, we act as citizens, we have the law, according to which we judge a man to be a good or a bad citizen; and insofar as we act as Italians, we have certain basic standards in the area of customs, manners and speech by which whatever we do as Italians is weighed and measured. Now the highest of those standards governing things specifically Italian are not peculiar to any one city of Italy, but common to them all, and among these can be counted the vernacular we have been seeking, the vernacular whose scent is in every city but whose lair is in none.

(*De vulgari eloquentia* I.xvi.3–4)

while on the other we have the "astripetal" passage of the second book, scarcely less than rapturous in its sense of the vernacular utterance under its now rhetorical and musical aspect as that whereby the poet rejoices in the aquiline – or dare we say it wingèd (*Ali*ghieri) – substance of his own now consummate humanity:

> Caveat ergo quilibet et discernat ea que dicimus; et quando hec tria pure cantare intendit, vel que ad ea directe ac pure secuntur, prius Elicone potatus, tensis fidibus ad supremum, secure plectrum tum movere incipiat. Sed cautionem atque discretionem hanc accipere, sicut decet, hic opus et labor est, quoniam nunquam sine strenuitate ingenii et artis assiduitate scientiarumque habitu fieri potest. Et hii sunt quos Poeta Eneidorum sexto Dei dilectos et ab ardente virtute sublimatos ad ethera deorumque filios vocat, quanquam figurate loquatur. Et ideo confutetur illorum stultitia qui, arte scientiaque immunes, de solo ingenio confidentes, ad summa summe canenda prorumpunt; et a tanta presumptuositate desistant; et si anseres natura vel desidia sunt, nolint astripetam aquilam imitari.

Let all alike take care therefore and note clearly what we are saying here, namely that anyone intending to sing of these three things, either in themselves or as regards those things directly and straightforwardly flowing from them, must before confidently taking up the plectrum first drink of Helicon and tune every string of his lyre to perfection. But the real hard work here lies in learning how properly to exercise caution and judgement, something that can never be achieved without constant effort, application and acquisition in the areas both of art and of science. And such are those whom the poet in *Aeneid* VI calls beloved of the gods, raised to heaven by valiant, eager striving, and sons of gods, although he is but speaking figuratively. And thus is shown up and confounded the folly of those who, untouched by art or knowledge and trusting solely in their own wit, rush in and presume to sing of the highest things in the highest style. Let them desist from such presumption, and, if they are geese by nature or idleness, let them not wish to imitate the eagle that seeks the stars.

(*De vulgari eloquentia* II.iv.9–10)

Now Dante's, in the *De vulgari eloquentia*, is, as he himself says (I.i.1), a rich hydromel ("ydromellum") of precedents and influences, precedents and influences countenancing as far as the literary-aesthetic sensibility of Book II is concerned all the main representatives of the rhetorical tradition going back via the late medieval authors of the *poetriae* (Geoffrey of Vinsauf, for example, John of Garland and Matthew of Vendôme) to Aristotle, Cicero and Quintilian in the ancient world. Everything from the *genera dicendi* to the *gradus constructionis* and on to the fine points of lexis, rhythm and rhyme are present and correct, Dante again, then, both amply reflecting and fully honouring the tradition in which he stands. But more important for the interpretation of his treatise than his allegiances are his initiatives, for the *De vulgari eloquentia*, whatever else it is, is a countenancing of the rhetorical tradition from the point of view of one grasped by the ascendancy of existence over essence, a situation into which language as represented in the case of Dante by his again beloved *lingua di sì* in its now illustrious complexion enters as a principle both of preliminary and of ultimate affirmation, as that whereby the soul is brought forth from the abyss of unrecognizability and inaccessibility. Nothing less than this will do as an account of what in truth is going on in the *De vulgari eloquentia*, for nothing less than this gives adequate expression to Dante's sense of the word as that whereby this or that instance of specifically human being knows itself in its actuality, as *there* in keeping with its innermost reasons. Nothing less than this does justice to its 'serietà terribile', to its taking up of the merely cultural in all the contingency thereof in what actually and ultimately matters about it.

THE TRIUMPH OF THE IMAGE AND A WRITERLY TEXT

But that is not all; for it is a question in Dante, not merely of language in general as the means of historical and indeed of eschatological self-presencing in human experience, but of the image in particular (*a*) as finessing the proposition pure and simple as the way of ontological disclosure, and (*b*) as apt in its endless suggestivity to confirm the status of the reader as party to the entire undertaking, as there alongside the writer for the purposes not merely of determining but of generating that meaning in the first place. To take, then, the first of these things, namely the primordial power of the image as the means of disclosure, we need only open the text at its first page – the text here being the *Commedia* as but Dante's point of arrival in this respect – to be impressed by its status and function not as a *product* but as a *principle* of ontic intelligence, as that whereby we are at once initiated in a sense of the *how it stands and how it fares* with the individual in the moment of his self-losing as a creature of ultimate accountability:

> Nel mezzo del cammin di nostra vita
> mi ritrovai per una selva oscura,
> ché la diritta via era smarrita.
> Ahi quanto a dir qual era è cosa dura
> esta selva selvaggia e aspra e forte
> che nel pensier rinova la paura!
> Tant' è amara che poco è più morte;
> ma per trattar del ben ch'i' vi trovai,
> dirò de l'altre cose ch'i' v'ho scorte.
> Io non so ben ridir com' i' v'intrai,
> tant' era pien di sonno a quel punto
> che la verace via abbandonai.

In the middle of the journey of our life I came to myself in a dark wood where the straight way was lost. Ah, how hard

a thing it is to tell of that wood, savage and harsh and dense,
the thought of which renews my fear! So bitter is it that death
is hardly more. But to give account of the good that I found
in that place I will tell of the other things I came upon there.
I cannot rightly say how I entered into it, so full of sleep was I
at that moment when I left the true way.

(*Inferno* I.1–12)

Morally the situation here – turning as it always does in Dante
upon the notion of love-garnering, of bringing home one kind of
love to another – is plain. Called in the way we have seen to reach
out for the *what might be* of self on the planes of properly human
knowing and loving, the soul has delivered itself to the alternative
project, whence it knows itself by way only of the inexplicability of
it all. But that is not where Dante begins. Rather, he begins with
the image – with the forest Wanderweg – as at once transcending
the analytical power of the proposition pure and simple. True, the
analytical moment follows on just about immediately, Dante going
out of his way to confirm the whole thing as but an instance of
spiritual somnambulance. But by that stage, and thanks to the
image as his first port of call, we are already party to an act of
spiritual intelligence, already *au fait* with the trauma and the terror
of it all. And what applies on the threshold of this first canticle
of the poem applies throughout, the image forever rejoicing in its
status as preliminary – and indeed as permanently on hand – as the
way of psycho-ontological elucidation, of laying open the twofold
substance and sensation of being in its proximity to non-being.
Consider, for example, these lines (52–57) from *Inferno* III, the
canto of the *ignavi* or – by way either of their restlessness or
indifference – the insignificantly busy:

> E io, che riguardai, vidi una 'nsegna
> che girando correva tanto ratta,
> che d'ogne posa mi parea indegna;
> e dietro le venìa sì lunga tratta

di gente, ch'i' non averei creduto
che morte tanta n'avesse disfatta.

And I looked and saw a whirling banner that ran so fast that
it seemed as if impatient of all rest, and behind it came so long
a train of people that I should never have believed death had
undone so many.

or these (lines 31–33 and 40–45) from *Inferno* V, the canto of the
adulterous or intemperate in love:

La bufera infernal, che mai non resta,
mena li spirti con la sua rapina;
voltando e percotendo li molesta.
        …
E come li stornei ne portan l'ali
nel freddo tempo, a schiera larga e piena,
così quel fiato li spiriti mali
    di qua, di là, di giù, di sù li mena;
nulla speranza li conforta mai,
    non che di posa, ma di minor pena.

The infernal storm, never resting, seizes and drives the spirits
before it; smiting and whirling them about, it torments them.
And just as, in the chilly season, starlings are borne aloft by
their wings in a flock as ample as it is dense so likewise does
that blast buffet the wicked spirits.

or these (lines 10–15) from *Inferno* XXXIV as bearing upon
treachery in its now pure form:

Già era, e con paura il metto in metro,
là dove l'ombre tutte eran coperte,
e trasparien come festuca in vetro.
    Altre sono a giacere; altre stanno erte,
quella col capo e quella con le piante;
altra, com' arco, il volto a' piè rinverte.

I was already there – and with fear I set it down in verse – where the shades were wholly covered and showed through like straws in glass; some were lying, some erect, this with the head, that with the soles uppermost, another like a bow, bent face to feet.

– where in each case it is by way of the image that the leading idea – to wit, the making over of self despite self to the means of its moral and ontological undoing and this as a matter of infinite sadness – is confirmed in point both of the *what* and of the *how* of its positive living out, by way of its notional and of its psychological substance. Thus called upon to shape and substantiate its existence in the light of what actually and ultimately matters about it, the soul settles instead for a frantic but fundamentally aimless progression from one self-consciously inauthentic possibility to another (the *Inferno* III passage). Called upon to love and to love amply, but at the same time to gather in every contingent impulse of the spirit to the love given with existence itself, it knows itself only in the drivenness thereof, in the hither-and-thither restlessness of the sensitive soul (the *Inferno* V passage). And called upon to affirm itself by way of the kind of transhumanity as but humanity itself in act, and thus of the constant creativity and recreativity thereof, it subsists by way only of the most complete kind of spiritual stasis, of the twofold lovelessness and lifelessness of being in its proximity to non-being (the *Inferno* XXXIV passage). But that again is not what Dante says, his, at every stage, being a trusting of the idea to the image – to the whirling banner, to the tempest and to the frozen contortion of the human form – as uniquely adequate to the matter in hand, as that whereby both he and his reader as but fellow travellers enter into the deepest and darkest places of the spirit as astray, of being in its 'unlikeness'.

And what applies to being in its proximity to non-being, to its living on in the 'region of dissimilitude', applies also to being in its homecoming, the image once again conveying – but, more than this, confirming in its otherwise unspeakable substance and intensity – the exhilaration of it all, the rapt sensation of proper emergence; so, for example, on the threshold of the *Purgatorio* as the canticle of spiritual emancipation, a skyscape suggesting precisely the splendour and spaciousness thereof, the notion of emancipation thus understood as but a matter of blessed ulteriority:

> Dolce color d'orïental zaffiro,
> che s'accoglieva nel sereno aspetto
> del mezzo, puro infino al primo giro,
>   a li occhi miei ricominciò diletto,
> tosto ch'io usci' fuor de l'aura morta
> che m'avea contristati li occhi e 'l petto.
>   Lo bel pianeto che d'amar conforta
> faceva tutto rider l'orïente,
> velando i Pesci ch'erano in sua scorta.
>   I' mi volsi a man destra, e puosi mente
> a l'altro polo, e vidi quattro stelle
> non viste mai fuor ch'a la prima gente.
>   Goder pareva 'l ciel di lor fiammelle:
> oh settentrïonal vedovo sito,
> poi che privato se' di mirar quelle!

The sweet hue of oriental sapphire which was gathering upon the serene face of the heavens pure even to the first circle gladdened my eyes again as soon as I passed out of the dead air that had afflicted my eyes and breast. The fair planet that prompts to love caused the orient in its entirety to laugh, veiling as it did so the fishes that were in her train. I turned to the right and set my mind on the other pole, and saw four stars never seen before but by the first people, the sky seeming to rejoice in their sparkling. Oh widowed region of the north, you who are denied that sight!

(*Purgatorio* I.13–27)

while on the threshold of the *Paradiso,* and suggestive now, not merely of the splendour and spaciousness of it all, of the substance

and sensation of drawing nigh on the plane of properly human
being, but of these things in, so to say, their nth degree, the "day
added unto day" sequence of Canto I:

> Fatto avea di là mane e di qua sera
> tal foce, e quasi tutto era là bianco
> quello emisperio, e l'altra parte nera,
>   quando Beatrice in sul sinistro fianco
> vidi rivolta e riguardar nel sole:
> aguglia sì non li s'affisse unquanco.
>   E sì come secondo raggio suole
> uscir del primo e risalire in suso,
> pur come pelegrin che tornar vuole,
>   così de l'atto suo, per li occhi infuso
> ne l'imagine mia, il mio si fece,
> e fissi li occhi al sole oltre nostr' uso.
>   Molto è licito là, che qui non lece
> a le nostre virtù, mercé del loco
> fatto per proprio de l'umana spece.
>   Io nol soffersi molto, né sì poco,
> ch'io nol vedessi sfavillar dintorno,
> com' ferro che bogliente esce del foco;
>   e di sùbito parve giorno a giorno
> essere aggiunto, come quei che puote
> avesse il ciel d'un altro sole addorno.

That same passage had brought morning there and evening
here when – with just about all the hemisphere beyond lit
up, the rest, however, still darkling – I saw Beatrice turned to
her left and (though never did eagle look so fixedly upon it)
gazing upon the sun. And even as, like a pilgrim who wishes
to return, a second ray is wont to issue from the first there
to mount up once more, so from her action, imprinted by
way of my eyes upon my imagining, mine too was inclined,
I likewise fixing my eyes upon the sun beyond our custom.
Much is granted there which here, by virtue of the place made

for the human race as its rightful place, is denied our proper
power, and so not long did I endure it, though nor so little
that I did not see it sparkle round about like iron that issues
boiling from the fire. And there upon a sudden, day seemed to
be added to day, as if he who is able had adorned the heaven
with another sun.

(Paradiso I.43–63)

Everywhere, then, the pattern is the same, for everywhere it is a
question of what in truth amounts to something approaching
a revised sense of proper predication, of the logical conditions
governing the qualification of this *x* by this *y*. Gone in other words
is any sense of the image as a matter merely of semantic shift
(*metaphor*) or of analogy (*simile*) and of this as accountable to the
plain sense of the text. For with what in Dante amounts to a steady
referral of essence to existence, of the idea pure and simple to the
twofold agony and ecstasy of its living out as a principle of self-
actualization on the part of the one who says 'I', the image and the
image alone commends itself as equal to the matter in hand, and
this by way not merely – indeed not at all – of *exornatio* or deft
elaboration but of primordiality.

But with this – with what amounts in Dante to a privileging
of the image rather than the idea as the in-and-through-which
of ontological awareness – we are still not quite home where the
triumph of the *Commedia* is concerned; for this privileging of the
image as uniquely adequate to discourse on the plane of existence,
to the agony and ecstasy of man's actually *being there* as man, goes
hand in hand with a co-involvement of the reader when it comes,
not merely to the elucidation, but to the very substantiation of the
text in point of its in truth limitless power to signify. Eloquent
already, then, in respect of the 'co-involvement of the reader'
aspect of the argument are Dante's famous addresses to the
ubiquitous 'lettore' of the text, addresses designed straightaway
to liquidate the notion of mere spectatorship on his or her part,
of the merely passive presence of reader to writer; so, for example,

the "Se tu se' or, lettore, a creder lento / ciò ch'io dirò" moment
of *Inferno* XXV:

> Se tu se' or, lettore, a creder lento
> ciò ch'io dirò, non sarà maraviglia,
> ché io che 'l vidi, a pena il mi consento.
>   Com' io tenea levate in lor le ciglia,
> e un serpente con sei piè si lancia
> dinanzi a l'uno, e tutto a lui s'appiglia.

Should, reader, you be slow to credit what I shall now tell, 'tis
no wonder, for I who saw it can scarcely consent myself. With
my eyes, then, firmly fixed upon them, lo, a six-footed serpent
thrusts up before one of them and lays hold of him whole.

(*Inferno* XXV.46–51)

or the "Com' io divenni allor gelato e fioco / nol dimandar, lettor"
moment of *Inferno* XXXIV:

> Quando noi fummo fatti tanto avante,
> ch'al mio maestro piacque di mostrarmi
> la creatura ch'ebbe il bel sembiante,
>   d'innanzi mi si tolse e fé restarmi,
> "Ecco Dite", dicendo, "ed ecco il loco
> ove convien che di fortezza t'armi".
>   Com' io divenni allor gelato e fioco,
> nol dimandar, lettor, ch'i' non lo scrivo,
> però ch'ogne parlar sarebbe poco.
>   Io non mori' e non rimasi vivo;
> pensa oggimai per te, s'hai fior d'ingegno,
> qual io divenni, d'uno e d'altro privo.

When we had gone on so far that my master thought it good
to show me the creature who was once so fair he stepped aside
as my leader and bid me stop, saying: "Behold Dis, for this
is the place you must take courage as your breastplate." How

then, at once frozen and fainthearted I became, do not ask, O reader, for words – all of them – would fall short, for I died not nor did I remain alive. Provided only you have the wit, think now for yourself what I became, denied as I was both life and death.

(Inferno XXXIV.16–27)

or the "Or ti riman, lettor, sovra 'l tuo banco" moment of *Paradiso* X:

> Or ti riman, lettor, sovra 'l tuo banco,
> dietro pensando a ciò che si preliba,
> s'esser vuoi lieto assai prima che stanco.
>   Messo t'ho innanzi: omai per te ti ciba;
> ché a sé torce tutta la mia cura
> quella materia ond' io son fatto scriba.

Stay now, reader, on your bench, thinking over the things of which you have had now a foretaste, and 'ere you are weary you'll have much delight. My table I have set out before you, but feed now yourself, for the matter of which I am made scribe bends to itself my every care.

(Paradiso X.22–27)

or, as bearing now, not so much on the *message* as on the *mechanism* of the text, on its now exquisitely calibrated artistry, the "Aguzza qui, lettor, ben li occhi vero" moment of *Purgatorio* VIII:

> Aguzza qui, lettor, ben li occhi al vero,
> ché 'l velo è ora ben tanto sottile,
> certo che 'l trapassar dentro è leggero.

Here, then, reader, sharpen still further your eye for the truth, for so fine now is the veil that the passing through it is but a light matter.

(Purgatorio VIII.19–21)

or the "Lettor tu vedi ben com 'io innalzo / la mia matera" moment of *Purgatorio* IX:

> Lettor, tu vedi ben com' io innalzo
> la mia matera, e però con più arte
> non ti maravigliar s'io la rincalzo.

Here you may indeed discern, reader, how I raise still further my theme; wonder not, therefore, if with still greater art I secure it.

(*Purgatorio* IX.70–72)

or, superlatively (for never was strategy in the interests of seriousness so scintillating), the "per le note / di questa comedia, lettor, ti giuro" of *Inferno* XVI:

> Sempre a quel ver c'ha faccia di menzogna
> de' l'uom chiuder le labbra fin ch'el puote,
> però che sanza colpa fa vergogna;
>   ma qui tacer nol posso; e per le note
> di questa comedìa, lettor, ti giuro,
> s'elle non sien di lunga grazia vòte,
>   ch'i' vidi per quell' aere grosso e scuro
> venir notando una figura in suso,
> maravigliosa ad ogne cor sicuro,
>   sì come torna colui che va giuso
> talora a solver l'àncora ch'aggrappa
> o scoglio o altro che nel mare è chiuso,
>   che 'n sù si stende e da piè si rattrappa.

When it comes to the truth that has the face of a lie a man should always seal his lips as far as he is able, for otherwise, and without any fault of his own, it brings shame upon him. But here I cannot be silent, and by the strains of this Comedy – so may they not fail of lasting favour – I swear to you, reader, that I saw come swimming up through that gross and murky air a figure amazing even to the steadiest of souls, a figure just like one who, having gone down on occasion to loose the anchor caught on a reef or on something else in the sea, surfaces again, stretching upwards as he does so and readying his feet for the final stroke.

(*Inferno* XVI.124–36)

But – and this now is what matters – for all their addressing by turns both the message and the mechanism of the text, these appeals on Dante's part to the reader reach down way beyond their surface civility; for built into the very fabric of the *Commedia*, into its proceeding by way of the image as the in-and-through-which of spiritual intelligence, is an invitation to reflect upon it with a view to filling out and indeed to fashioning its inner and abiding meaning, to – in effect and indeed in very truth – a coming alongside Dante himself as party to the entire undertaking. Here, then, there can be no looking the other way or passing by on the other side, for what we have here is a triumph *avant la lettre* of writerliness over readerliness as a way of seeing and setting up the literary project, a systematic co-implication of the cherished 'lettore' at the point of ultimate concern.

CONCLUSION:

IN CONVERSATION WITH DANTE

To enter into conversation with another person – to engage, that is to say, in the kind of 'turn and turn about sharing' whereby one individual seeks to stand significantly in the presence of another – is to do various things. It is (*a*) to discern and duly to acknowledge the kind of otherness – be it the otherness either of temperament or of circumstance or of both – making in the next man for the distinctive utterance; (*b*) to allow the exchange in some sense and in some degree to put self into question; and (*c*) if not necessarily to acquiesce in what has been said, then at least to seek out and to confirm as far as may be a common horizon of concern, a something somewhere serving to quicken and sustain the whole undertaking. And what applies with respect to the face-to-face encounter applies *a fortiori* to the historical encounter, where again it is a question of reaching out and, if only by way of a movement of imagination, of recovering as far as may be a set or subset of preoccupations transcending their cultural conditioning, this and this alone ensuring the aforesaid *in-youing* and *in-meing* of those genuinely engaged one with another on the plane of properly human being.

What, then, of Dante, of, more precisely, Dante *then* and *now*?

Dante, to begin with the otherness of it all, was every inch a product of the pre-humanistic and high-scholastic period in which he lived, moved and had his being. On the one hand, then, there were his classical *auctores* with to the fore among them Virgil, Ovid, Horace, Statius and Lucan, each after his manner equipping him for his proper destiny as a poet and prophet. On the other hand there were his Christian *auctores* from Augustine via the Victorines and Cistercians through to the scholastic luminaries represented magisterially by the likes of Albert the Great, Thomas Aquinas and Bonaventure, each after his manner decisive for Dante's reconstruction of the substance and psychology of the religious life. All this, then, and more besides, by way of the otherness of it all, of the forces at work both from beyond and from within making for his eminently situated humanity, for his status as a child of his time.

But – and this now is what matters – Dante's, for all his delighting in the company of those poets, philosophers and theologians decisive for the shaping and substantiation of his own unique presence in the world, was a steady bringing home of the idea pure and simple to the act of existence as apt to transcend each and every specifically cultural inflexion of the spirit, every high-level concern apt to determine its precise complexion. And the outcome of this? A discourse that without prejudice to the particularity of, again, his own unique and uniquely precious presence in the world, reaches out to all those likewise anxious in respect of the innermost meaning of it all, of what actually matters about their *being there* as creatures of ultimate accountability.

Quid plus, then? What more is there to say and to do other than to rejoice in the presence of one who, having sung a song of ascents, looks to converse with all those willing to lend an ear? Little indeed but to reply in kind.

FURTHER READING

Given the exponential growth of Dante bibliography the best that can be done here is to offer the reader a bare minimum, just enough to get started. Given also, however, that Dante is far and away his best interpreter a bare minimum is perhaps all that is required, an attentive reading of the text being enough to confirm the reader in a sense of what actually matters about it. What follows, then, is a selection of books in English designed to offer a preliminary account of the *who, when, what* and *where* of his life and works, and an indication of texts and translations – restricted for the moment to the *Vita nova*, the *Convivio*, the *De vulgari eloquentia* and the *Commedia* as the pillars, so to speak, of our current meditation – for the benefit of those anxious to deepen the encounter. Almost without exception they each of them offer a more ample bibliography.

LIFE AND WORKS

Anderson, William, *Dante the Maker*, London: Routledge & Kegan Paul, 1980.

Barbi, Michele, *Life of Dante* (ed. and trans. by Paul G. Ruggiers), Berkeley: University of California Press, 1954 (originally *Vita di Dante*, Florence: Sansoni, 1933 and 1965).

Bemrose, Stephen, *A New Life of Dante*, Exeter: University of Exeter Press, 2000 (revised edn 2014).

Caesar, Michael (ed.), *Dante: The Critical Heritage 1314(?)–1870*, London and New York: Routledge, 1989.

Hainsworth, Peter and Robey, David, *Dante: A Very Short Introduction*, Oxford: Oxford University Press, 2015.

Havely, Nick, *Dante*, Malden, MA: Blackwell Publishing, 2007.

Hawkins, Peter S., *Dante: A Brief History*, Malden, MA and Oxford: Blackwell, 2006.

Hollander, Robert, *Dante: A Life in Works*, New Haven, CT and London: Yale University Press, 2001.

Holmes, George, *Dante*, Oxford: Clarendon Press, 1980.

Jacoff, Rachel (ed.), *The Cambridge Companion to Dante*, 2nd edn, Cambridge: Cambridge University Press, 2007.

Reynolds, Barbara, *Dante: The Poet, the Political Thinker, the Man*, London: I.B. Tauris, 2006.

Santagata, Marco, *Dante: The Story of his Life*, trans. Richard Dixon, Cambridge, MA: Harvard University Press (The Belknap Press), 2016 (from the Italian *Dante: il romanzo della sua vita*, Milan: Mondadori, 2012).

Scott, John Alfred, *Understanding Dante*, Notre Dame, IN: University of Notre Dame Press, 2004.

Shaw, Prue, *Reading Dante: From Here to Eternity*: New York: Liveright, 2014.

Took, John, *Dante: Lyric Poet and Philosopher: An Introduction to the Minor Works*, Oxford: Clarendon Press, 1990.

Took, John, *Dante*, Princeton, NJ: Princeton University Press, 2020.

Toynbee, Paget, *Dante Alighieri: His Life and Works*, New York: Dover Publications, 2005 (from the fourth edition of 1910, originally 1900, with an introduction by Robert Hollander).

TEXTS AND TRANSLATIONS

Vita Nuova, ed. Domenico De Robertis in *Dante Alighieri: Opere minori*, vol. I, part 1, Milan and Naples: Riccardo Ricciardi Editore, 1984, 1–247.

Vita Nova, ed. Luca Carlo Rossi, with an introduction by Guglielmo Gorni, Milan: Mondadori, 1999.

Vita Nuova, ed. Jennifer Petrie and June Salmons, Dublin: Belfield Italian Library, 1994.

La Vita Nuova (Poems of Youth), translation with an introduction by Barbara Reynolds, Harmondsworth: Penguin Books, 1969 (with reprints).

Convivio, ed. Cesare Vasoli and Domenico De Robertis, in *Dante Alighieri: Opere minori*, vol. I, part 2, Milan and Naples: Riccardo Ricciardi Editore, 1988.

Il Convivio, ed. Maria Simonelli, Bologna: Pàtron, 1966.

Il Convivio, ed. Giovanni Busnelli and Giuseppe Vandelli, 2 vols, Florence: Felice Le Monnier, 1968, with an introduction by Michele Barbi and a revised bibliography by Antonio Enzo Quaglio (volumes 4 and 5 of the *Opere di Dante* directed by Michele Barbi).

The Banquet, trans. Christopher J. Ryan, Saratoga, CA: Anma Libri, 1989.

Dante's Il Convivio (*The Banquet*), trans. Richard H. Lansing, New York and London: Garland, 1990.

De vulgari eloquentia, ed. Pier Vincenzo Mengaldo, in *Dante Alighieri: Opere minori*, vol. II, Milan and Naples: Riccardo Ricciardi Editore, 1979, 1–237.

De vulgari eloquentia, ed. Aristide Marigo, 3rd edn, Florence: Felice Le Monnier, 1968 (volume 6 of the *Opere di Dante* directed by Michele Barbi).

De vulgari eloquentia: Dante's Book of Exile, trans. Marianne Shapiro, Lincoln, NE and London: University of Nebraska Press, 1990.

De vulgari eloquentia, ed. and trans. Steven Botterill, Cambridge: Cambridge University Press, 1996.

La Commedia secondo l'antica vulgata, ed. Giorgio Petrocchi, 4 vols, Milan: Mondadori, 1966–67 (Edizione Nazionale a cura della Società Dantesca Italiana).

La Divina Commedia, ed. Natalino Sapegno, 3 vols, Florence: La Nuova Italia, 1968.

La Divina Commedia, ed. Umberto Bosco and Giovanni Reggio, 3 vols, Florence: Le Monnier, 1979.

The Divine Comedy of Dante Alighieri, trans. Charles Eliot Norton, 3 vols, Boston and New York: The Riverside Press, 1892 (various reprints).

The Divine Comedy, Italian text with translation by John D. Sinclair, 3 vols, New York: Oxford University Press, 1939 and 1961 (with reprints).

The Divine Comedy, translated with a commentary by Charles S. Singleton, 6 vols, Princeton, NJ: Princeton University Press, 1970 (published in England by Routledge & Kegan Paul, 1971).

The Divine Comedy, translated with an introduction, notes and commentary by Mark Musa, 3 vols, Bloomington, IN: Indiana University Press, 1997–2005.

The Divine Comedy, trans. Allen Mandelbaum (with an introduction by Eugenio Montale and notes by Peter Armour), New York, London and Toronto: Alfred A. Knopf, 1995.

The Divine Comedy, trans. Robin Kirkpatrick, 3 vols, London: Penguin Books, 2006– (combined in one volume with a revised introduction, 2012).

INDEX OF NAMES

NOTE ON THE AUTHOR

John Took is Professor Emeritus of Dante Studies at University College London. Prominent among his books and articles on Dante – many of them turning on the poet's significance as a leading representative of what Paul Tillich calls the 'existentialist point of view' in philosophy and theology – is his recently published intellectual biography of Dante entitled simply *Dante* (Princeton University Press, 2020).

NOTE ON THE TYPE

The text of this book is set in Adobe Caslon, named after the English punch-cutter and type-founder William Caslon I (1692–1766). Caslon's rather old-fashioned types were modelled on seventeenth-century Dutch designs, but found wide acceptance throughout the English-speaking world for much of the eighteenth century until replaced by newer types towards the end of the century. Used in 1776 to print the Declaration of Independence, they were revived in the nineteenth century and have been popular ever since, particularly amongst fine printers. There are several digital versions, of which Carol Twombly's Adobe Caslon is one.